# BEYOND THE BORDERS

*By the same author*

A Breath of Border Air
Another Breath of Border Air
A Border Bairn
God Bless the Borders!
Lady of the Manse
A Mouse in the Manse

LAVINIA DERWENT

# Beyond the Borders

*Illustrated by Elizabeth Haines*

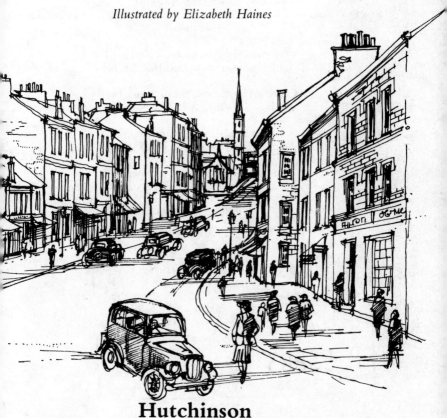

**Hutchinson**
London Melbourne Auckland Johannesburg

Century Hutchinson Ltd, Brookmount House, 62–65 Chandos Place, London WC2N 4NW

Century Hutchinson Australia Pty Ltd
PO Box 496, 16–22 Church Street. Hawthorn, Victoria 3122, Australia

Century Hutchinson New Zealand Ltd
PO Box 40–086, Glenfield, Auckland 10, New Zealand

Century Hutchinson South Africa Pty Ltd
PO Box 337, Bergvlei, 2012 South Africa

Phototypeset in Linotron Bembo
by Input Typesetting Ltd, London

Printed and bound in Great Britain by
Anchor Brendon Ltd, Tiptree, Essex

ISBN 0 09 173444 4

For the late Sir William Collins
('Good Old Billy') with affection and gratitude

# Contents

1   Leaving the Nest                    1

2   Finding My Feet                     9

3   It's Only For a Fortnight          19

4   Home Truths                        25

5   Ready! Steady! GO!                 32

6   Digging In                         47

7   Settling Down                      57

8   Finding my Feet Again              68

9   Leisure and Pleasure               77

10  The Literary Scene                 86

11  Scattered Showers                  95

12  Foreign Fields                    104

13  Flight Into Egypt                 115

14  King of Cairo                     127

15  Back to Reality                   141

16  The World My Oyster               152

*Envoi*                               164

# 1 Leaving the Nest

It all began with the exciting sound of the telephone ringing in our isolated farmhouse.

'Telly-phone!'

Jessie, the odd-job woman, had come to the
door and was shouting to me at the pitch of her
voice. She was forced to shout for I was sitting
in the swing under the big tree oblivious to the
outside world. I had been reading an old copy
of *Hiawatha* and my head was so full of its
cadences that I almost answered in like vein.

> Hear the telephone, mighty telephone
> Calling loudly o'er the wires.
> Who is calling, tell me, Jessie. . . ?

'Telly-phone!'

This time the voice was so angry I shook
myself into the here-and-now and called back:

1

'Coming, Jessie. Who is it?' It would likely be the sheep-dip man or Bella from the post office with some local gossip.

'Dinna ken!' grunted Jessie and stamped back into the house.

Jessie hated the telephone. It was a noisy beast and she would answer it only in an emergency. Today I was the only one at home. Father and Mother had gone off on a jaunt over the Border to attend a farm sale, which Jessie called a *roup*. According to her, going over the Border meant penetrating into enemy territory, for she was still at loggerheads with our old adversaries, the English. She was cross with my parents for going, cross with the telephone for ringing, cross with me for not rushing to answer it; but Jessie thrived on rage. It was like a stimulant that pepped her up.

Since ever I could remember Jessie had ruled the kitchen, scolded the servant girls, cooked nourishing meals, mended and knitted, coped with all emergencies and – cross or not – been my lifeline when I was a bairn. It was to her apron I had clung for comfort when other grown-ups had no time to bother about me, and it was her voice I liked best to hear especially if she was telling me a story in the byre while she was milking the cows.

'A'weel! There was once a wee centipede called Meggy-Mony-Feet . . .' Jessie's stories were all about 'beasts' and all in the dialect. English was a foreign language to her.

When I went into the house she was holding the receiver at arm's length as if it would bite

2

her. 'It's a tellygram on the 'phone,' she said grumpily; and now that she had done her duty slammed it back on its cradle, cutting us off from the world.

'Jessie!' I cried indignantly. 'If it was a telegram it must be important. And now we'll never know.'

Yes, we would.

The telephone rang immediately and Bella from the post office informed me there was a telegram awaiting delivery.

'Who is it for?'

'For you, lassie.'

'Me!'

I was trembling with excitement, and though Bella read the telegram several times, it was ages before I could take it in. Yes! it *was* addressed to me from a publisher in Glasgow asking me to come for an interview the day after tomorrow. To Glasgow!

'I'll send it up wi' the Postie,' Bella was telling me, and having dealt with the telegram went on to talk about her bunion and the cat that had just kittened. 'Fower torty-shells. Ye'll no' be wantin' one?' she asked hopefully. No! we had hundreds already – well, dozens – running spare about the farm.

'A'weel!' sighed Bella. 'I'd better get on.'

Me, too! But I was in such a dazed state I didn't know how to get on.

I remembered the advertisement I had seen in the *Scotsman* a few days ago and how on an impulse I had answered it in my best hand-writing. I had acquired a third-hand typewriter

3

by now, an elderly Oliver which stuck after every few words leaving a trail of smudges on the paper. A sinister-sounding bell rang at the end of each line, always taking me by surprise and startling me out of my skin; so after a few messy attempts I abandoned the typewriter and took to my fountain pen.

'Dear Sir or Madam!' I began, not knowing how to address a publishing firm. The advertisement had stated tersely that a caption-writer was required for a fortnight in a publishing house. Apply Box Number.

I had no hope of getting a reply and no notion what a caption-writer was; but it had something to do with writing, and in the unlikely event of my being chosen I could learn all about publishing in a fortnight. A fortnight! Little did I know!

I had reached the conclusion it was time I stopped wasting my time in limbo-land. For months I had been running wild around the farm enjoying my freedom after the restricting life I had been leading as a temporary Lady of the Manse. Now that my brother was safely married and a proper lady had taken over my duties I was FREE. Hooray! I could kick up my heels, forget about propriety and best of all have time to myself for reading and writing. At first it all went to my head.

But the sweet taste of freedom was beginning to turn sour, for it was not total freedom. Now that I was back home, I was under the restrictions of Mother's edicts and of Jessie's hard hand. I had submitted to them in the past, but since I had been out of the nest I was no longer so meek and biddable. I had acquired a modicum of independence and enough commonsense to think for myself, so I was beginning to see that Mother and Jessie were not always right. And yet I found it difficult to 'speak back' to them. I was a Miss Nobody not sure of my place.

But at least I had done *something*. I had made my first broadcast for the BBC in Edinburgh; and never will I forget the terror of that terrible day.

Jessie had sent me off with her customary adage ringing in my ears: 'The back's aye made for the burden'; but today it did not stiffen me up. The very thought of my voice being heard over the air appalled me. I remember looking out of the train window on my way to Edinburgh and watching a woman hanging out her washing. 'Lucky thing!' I thought enviously. I would willingly have scrubbed the kitchen floor a dozen times rather than face the ordeal ahead.

The rails seemed to be singing, 'I can't do it! I can't do it!' Try as I would, I could not switch off and think of something else, with the result I was in a state of jitters by the time the train drew up at Waverley Station.

I wandered along Princes Street looking in at the shop windows but not seeing anything. 'I can't do it! I can't do it!' I listened for a voice saying 'Yes, you can!' but I could only hear the din of the Edinburgh traffic. Somehow my feet found their way to the BBC headquarters at Number 5 Queen Street where I arrived too soon. I walked past the building one way, then turned and walked past it the other way. 'I'll never go in. Never!'

A commissionaire gave me a doubtful look, then opened the door and ushered me straight into a studio where a brisk lady was busy rehearsing a group of young singers.

'Hullo! Sit down,' was all she said to me, indicating a sofa at the side of the studio.

I sat and shook. Was that tall thing in the middle of the room a microphone and would I have to stand in front of it to read my story? Everybody in the world would hear me including Jessie. Why not just speak to her? After all, *she* was the one who started me off writing stories . . .

I was terrible! Even now I shiver with shame when I think back to that stilted broadcast and hope it has long been erased from the BBC's archives.

But they had asked for more, so perhaps there could be a future for me if only I could 'learn my trade'.

So that was why I had answered the advertisement in the *Scotsman*.

I was fizzing with excitement when I reread the telegram for the dozenth time, after the Postie finally delivered it. But Jessie douched me with cold water, as if I was a broody hen.

'Ye'll no' likely get the job,' she said gloomily.

Inwardly I agreed with her, but the mere fact of being asked to come for an interview was enough to set me on fire. 'All expenses paid,' the telegram said. I was to present myself at a publishing firm called William Collins Sons & Company Ltd. 144 Cathedral Street Glasgow. Signed Editor.

I ran about in all directions collecting some of my published 'pieces', including my broadcast scripts, and packed them into a shabby attaché case which I had to fasten with string. I had never been in Glasgow before and hoped the climate was dry, for my everlasting Harris tweed coat 'ponged' when it got soaked. I wore my sensible brogues, and a tammy on my head, and thus equipped set off to make my mark in the wide world.

It was drizzling in Glasgow. Not only that; there was a dank fog hanging in the air which blotted out all street signs. Tramcars charged at me as I tried to cross their paths not knowing where I was going. 'William Collins Sons and Company Ltd. 144 Cathedral Street,' I kept muttering to myself. But I could see no sign of a Cathedral let alone a Cathedral *Street*.

In the end I was forced to speak to a stranger who bumped into me in the gloom. 'Could you tell me where I am, please?'

Instantly I was given my first taste of warm-hearted Glasgow. A voice answered: 'Where d'ye want to go, hen?' (*Hen*, I discovered, was a local form of endearment. All men were addressed as *Jimmy*, all females as *hen*.) When I told him, he grabbed my arm and turned me round. I was going in the opposite direction; but 'Never mind, hen!' He would walk with me till I reached my destination.

It was the first, but by no means the last time

I had reason to be grateful to Glaswegians for their ready help in time of trouble.

At the publisher's I was taken into a waiting-room where I sat and ponged till I was taken into another room – an office, I suppose – to be interviewed by two men. One spoke with an Oxford accent (he was a *real* Collins), the other with a Yorkshire tongue (he was a *real* editor).

I showed them the contents of my attaché case and tried to answer their questions. Then they sent me back to the waiting-room to sit and steam. Years later I learned they had sifted me out, along with a few others, from over a hundred applicants. (The rest were too highly qualified, demanding large salaries. I did not demand anything, having no notion about salaries; therefore, being cheap, I was worth a trial.)

Before long they called me back and said they would try me out. The salary would be two pounds, ten shillings per week. Would that be all right? Yes, thank you! Could I start on Monday? Of course! I was so excited I would have agreed to anything.

They said they would fix me up to stay 'till I looked around' in a modest hotel in Sauchiehall Street – the Waverley (no longer in existence) and sent me on my way, telling me they would expect to see me on Monday at eight-thirty sharp.

I could not find my way back to the station but what did that matter? I was walking on air instead of the puddles. I had achieved a job in a publishing house and begun my career.

## 2. Finding My Feet

Jessie gave me a rubber apron to wear in the office. She had as little notion as I of what an office would be like, but as I was going to *work* for my living she assumed it must have something to do with washing dishes.

The shepherd, Jock-the-herd, was all for sending me off with a stout stick to use as a weapon of defence. 'Ye're sure to get murdered,' he told me dolefully, having heard that Glasgow was full of thugs and razor-slashers.

'It's only for a fortnight,' I kept telling everyone. It would take much longer than that to murder me.

I scarcely ate or slept in the intervening time before setting out for my 'trial'. In the train I wondered what I would do with my rich salary. Fancy having all that money coming in every week! (It had not occurred to me that I would have to pay for my board and lodgings.) My first purchase, I promised myself, would be a *red* hat. I was fed up with the muted colours Mother always chose to tone down my red hair. But now that I was free and earning my own money, I could become a scarlet woman, if I wanted.

I spent a strange night in the Waverley Hotel in Sauchiehall Street in a back room looking out on nothing. I ate an evening meal at a little table in the dingy dining-room while groups of silent men sat at other little tables paying no attention to me or to each other. It was a temperance hotel so perhaps they were commercial travellers suffering from the lack of a more cheerful liquid than fizzy lemonade.

I toyed with the brown soup and soggy steak pie, then went upstairs to my back bedroom to suck some home-made treacle toffee. The sight of Jessie's rubber apron in my attaché case brought a lump to my throat but I hastily swallowed it with the toffee.

In the morning I was up long before the lark. It was pitch dark and the dim electric bulb in my bedroom did little to lighten the gloom. The reason, I discovered when I went out, was that a typical Glasgow peasouper was engulfing the city. Even with a sense of direction and a knowledge of my surroundings, I could never have found my way unaided to the office. 'Do I turn right or left?' I asked the doorman, trying not to swallow mouthfuls of the swirling fog. (I had to ask him the same question every day I spent in that dreary hotel.) On that first morning I was passed like a parcel from one kindly person to another before finally reaching Cathedral Street where I was given a timecard to prove I had arrived. The start of my life as an employee!

I was shown into a room which I presumed to be an office, given a table as a desk and left to my own devices. There were pens, pencils, ink and a blotting pad on the table as well as some writing paper. I would have liked to scribble on the paper in my usual way, jotting down my first impressions of Glasgow or even starting a story about a wee kitten being lost in the fog. But I must not think of working for myself. I was hired to work for others now. So I sat bolt upright, stared in front of me and awaited orders.

When the editor arrived, delayed by the fog, he showed me the book he was compiling, a vast volume of encyclopedic knowledge encompassing everything under the sun from Prehistoric Monsters to Famous Men of all Ages, packed with illustrations. I had to provide the information to go with the pictures, and the captions had to end neatly without any overlapping to spoil the look of the said illustrations. In some cases I had to provide three hundred words, in others as many as five hundred, depending on the size of the pictures. It would mean I would be forced to count not only the words but the spaces in between, so I was constantly having to discard a long word – *beautiful*, for example – and replace it with *nice* – or the other way round, in order to get my jigsaw to fit.

Oh Jessie! I wish I was wearing your apron and black-leading the kitchen range!

11

The first picture I was given was the Signs of the Zodiac. Five hundred words! The editor indicated shelves of books which I could consult if I was stuck. Oh yes! I was stuck; but I browsed amongst the books till I had extracted every detail about the zodiac, including the fact that I myself had been born under the sign of Pisces. (So I was a fishy character!) I then laboriously wrote and rewrote my first caption, carefully counting the words and spaces, deleting and adding where necessary. Finally I passed it to the editor.

All he said after perusing it was 'Fine!' and passed me another illustration to caption. Then another and another till my head was whirling with unrelated facts – and so the day went by.

I found sitting still difficult after being accustomed to romping around in the fresh air on the farm. I tried not to yawn and reminded myself I must concentrate on my work for which I was being paid a large salary. (This feeling that I must give an adequate return persisted for many a long year.)

It seemed that hours had passed before a female person knocked at the door and suggested that she should 'Take Miss D. to tea'. This was elevenses, I suppose. I had pins and needles when I rose to my feet and could scarcely follow Miss Tweedie to a hidey-hole where several other 'girls' were assembled round a giant teapot. I was given a cup and an Abernethy biscuit for which I had to pay a penny; then Miss Tweedie gave me a key and said she would show me to the 'place'. She would wait outside. None of us, she told me, could go to the place till we had borrowed the key from Bessie Somebody to whom it must be faithfully returned.

When I got back to the office I found the editor in full flood dictating dozens of letters to one of his secretaries. He had two – a senior and a junior – for whom he rang at intervals and who appeared from nowhere like ectoplasm. They had notebooks at the ready and several sharpened pencils in their hands, so that if the point of one broke they could quickly transfer to another. They sat meekly beside the boss as he turned over the letters on his desk, and kept their pencils poised ready to dash off: 'Dear Sir or Madam' as soon as he embarked on his dictation. How clever they were, I thought, when I sometimes took a sideways glance at their flying fingers! They did not write *words* but made mysterious symbols, page after page in their notebooks. Greek would have been easier for me to decipher.

As soon as the dictation was over they departed to their own mysterious region and returned later with the letters in neat folders for the editor to sign. Their typewriters must have been more efficient than my old Oliver, for rarely did they make a smudge, and more rarely a spelling mistake. If they did, the editor took pains to point it out to them as gently as possible; whereupon they blushed bright red and retired to retype the entire letter.

I could not help hearing snatches of these letters in between puzzling over my captions. Many were addressed to 'Dear Sir or Madam' and sometimes the editor handed the letter to the secretary for her to produce 'the usual reply'. (Clever thing, I thought!) But often the letters were addressed to *real* people whose literary names I recognized: 'Dear Mr Masefield' and 'Dear Miss Katherine Tynan', even 'Dear Mr Wells'. By the end of the day I would not have been surprised if I had heard the editor begin, 'Dear Mr Charles Dickens' or 'Dear Mr William Shakespeare'.

The end of the day did not come till nearly six o'clock when a closing bell rang and I walked stiffly back through the fog to my hotel. I was so exhausted I could scarcely swallow my Brown Windsor soup; elated, too, to think I had more or less mastered the art of writing captions. I felt I had earned today's salary.

It was Bessie Somebody who suggested I should go into digs.

'What's digs?' I asked her.

'Tuts!' She was appalled at my ignorance and explained that the Waverley Hotel, modest though it was, must be outside my range of expenditure. 'You need less expensive board and lodgings, so you'd better find a bed-sitter.'

So I set out to look for digs. It occurred to me it would be best to find accommodation near the office to avoid that complicated journey in the morning. I did not realize that Cathedral Street was in the Townhead district – *Toonheid* to the locals – a slum area at that time, and that the people hanging desolately in the doorways were unemployed men who had given up a hopeless search for work. I wandered aimlessly about and eventually found the Cathedral itself, but even *I* knew one could not 'dig' in that fine edifice.

Presently a man lounging outside a tenement asked what I was looking for.

'Digs,' I said hopefully.

He spat on the pavement and said, 'Come up the stair.'

I followed him 'up the stair' and found it was a communal staircase of cracked stone steps with dilapidated doorways on each side of the landings. Help! Did people actually *live* here? I had to step over squabbling children and snarling dogs as the man led me right to the top of the tenement.

'Mrs Murphy takes folk in,' he told me before clattering away down the stone stairs. Was he one of Jock-the-herd's razor-slashers, I wondered?

I did not have the courage to rap at Mrs Murphy's door but she opened it before I could retreat, a blowzy woman with tousled hair and no teeth. 'Are ye lookin' for a place? Come in!'

She led me to a fusty room with a broken window where the only furniture appeared to be an unmade bed.

'Oh! I don't think it would suit,' I began. Whereupon she adopted a belligerent attitude.

'You snobs!' she jeered. 'What are ye lookin' for? Buckingam Palace?'

'N-no!' I stammered. 'But I don't think . . .'

'Weel! Get oot ma hoose!' she bellowed, and pushed me out of the door.

I retraced my steps, past screaming children,

past fighting dogs, past the razor-slasher lounging at the entrance, and walked away as quickly as I could, but with no purpose.

Suddenly I bumped into a body in the gloom. It was Miss Tweedie from the office.

'What are *you* doing here?' she enquired in a surprised voice.

'Looking for digs.'

'Mercy! In Townhead!' She drew me towards a gaslamp and opened the evening paper she was carrying. 'You're in the wrong district for digs. You should be out West.'

'Where's that?'

'Look!' She was peering at the advertisements in the paper. 'Here's one near Charing Cross. That's more like the thing.'

She tore the advertisement out of the paper, pointed me in the right direction, and I walked all the way to Charing Cross, not trusting myself to board a tramcar in case it whisked me away to Auchenshuggle (which really *was* the name on one of the cars) or as far away as Timbuktu. But at last I found the right address. It was in a place called Holland Street where the houses, though not tenements, had all seen better days.

I rang the bell of Number 40 and it was a gentlemanly man, decayed like the house, who opened the door and spoke in a put-on refined accent.

Yes, he told me, there was a room to let, a bed-sitting-room. He took me along an uncarpeted hallway to show it to me, switching on lights as he went. I heard shrieks and bumps from downstairs where 'the family' had their being in the basement.

The bed-sitter itself seemed adequate. It had a bed, a table, an easy chair, a wardrobe, and an open fire waiting to be lit. The bathroom was next door (shared by all the family, I was to discover) with a stained bath that was never used and a monstrous heater called a geyser that did not work. But 'the missus' would bring me kettles of hot water, light the fire and make up the bed if I wanted to install myself straight away.

When it came to talking about terms and I was making stumbling enquiries, he called downstairs for the missus to come up. *She* was obviously the down-trodden worker and *he* the fancy-man who did all the talking, out of a job and relying on his wife to supply him with beer and cigarette money. She, poor thing, was bowed down by the weight of her responsibilities, but looked up to her man whom she considered a cut above her. His word was law; and as she spoke to me she kept looking at him for a confirming nod.

'Would twenty-five shillings a week be all right?' she wondered.

Her husband nodded. That would include full board: breakfast, dinner, high tea, and a late cup of cocoa if wanted. Another nod from the man. Twenty-five shillings from my salary of two pounds ten shillings? That would surely leave me with ample money for necessities, even luxuries like red hats.

So I said yes and, thankful to have settled the

deal, made my way back to the Waverley Hotel where I packed my few belongings ready to start a new life in digs.

# 3. It's Only For a Fortnight

It's only for a fortnight, I kept telling myself, sometimes in a mood of despair, sometimes regretting it would be over so soon.

I disliked living in digs, but I could push the discomfort into the background and concentrate on 'learning my trade'. Make the most of this fortnight, I reminded myself every day as I walked the weary length of Cathedral Street. Learn all you can and make yourself as useful as possible.

In my eagerness to show myself willing I would even have put on Jessie's apron and scrubbed the doorstep. The editor was rushed off his feet trying to get the encyclopedic job finished in time. I noticed he took work home every night, so I offered to do the same if it would be a help. 'Yes, thank you,' he said. It

would be a great help if I took a batch of proof
home to correct.

Home!

How could I think of that bleak bed-sitter a
*home*? After living in a rambling farmhouse an
from being a Lady of the Manse, I was nov
confined to four walls and one window with n
outlook except the backgreen. But I was to
busy poring over proofs to have time to look a
anything else. The proofs were long unmanage
able sheets which never seemed to be in consecu
tive order, and I was constantly peering – cross
eyed – from one of them to a guide book on
'how to make correct corrections'! Press on, I
kept telling myself; it's only for a fortnight
Meantime, let them see you can pull you
weight.

When I got back to the digs each evening the
fire was lit and Mrs Colman was hovering in th
hall waiting to produce my high tea. Get *tha*
over, was her attitude. Mrs Colman was a geniu
at producing the cheapest and most unappetising
meals it is possible to imagine. Her favourite –
not mine – was boiled cod dumped on a cold
plate and swimming in a watery sauce. It wa
accompanied by two slices of plain white bread
and a small dollop of butter, which on reflection
must have been margarine, for it had a strange
taste which I had never experienced before, and
a wee helping of 'jam' in a cracked saucer
Occasionally there was a stale bun which I could
have bounced on the floor like a rubber ball. A
large teapot full of stewed tea completed my
feast.

A meal scarcely fit for the gods. Yet, looking back I have sympathy with Mrs Colman and her kind who eked out their household budgets halfpenny by halfpenny and succeeded in keeping their heads above water while feeding their brood however meagrely.

At the best of times I was never a great guzzler, and the sight of Mrs Colman's cuisine took away what was left of my appetite. How to dispose of the left-overs was a pressing problem. I pushed them about on the plate trying to make it look as if I had eaten a good meal, but prod them as I would, they never vanished into thin air. Sometimes I wrapped up the currant buns to drop on the way to the office, or pushed up the window and flung the contents of my plate to the cats and dogs scrabbling about in the backgreen.

There was nothing green about the backgreen. The grass had been trodden down by so many feet that even the thistles were struggling for life. The green was a sizable square of wasteground used by the tenement wives for drying their clothes and by the men for hoarding goodness knows what in a derelict shed at one corner.

There must have been a rota, I suppose, for the clothes drying, but it never seemed to work, for I heard constant squabbles about whose turn it was to use the clothes – rope. The voices grew louder as tempers frayed and the wives flung mouthfuls of angry words at each other. I used to draw back from the window as if dodging the blows, and felt that if Jessie had been here *she* would have sorted out their problems in no time.

Sometimes the backgreen was squelching with

mud, and when a sudden downpour of rain came on there was a rush to rescue the washing before it got soaked through. The next thing I heard was the screech of pulleys being pulled up in the kitchens where the clothes would eventually dry. If they were left outside for any length of time they became dirtier than before they were washed, for sooty smuts from surrounding chimneys blew down on them and sometimes stray dogs tried to tug them off the line.

But often the backgreen was alive with the sound of 'music'. Buskers appeared playing banjos or jew's-harps, others belted out raucous songs, coughing pathetically in the middle of 'Over the Sea to Skye'. Sometimes there would be a duo, one playing the music while the other did a kind of kick-up dance on the muddy ground.

Now and again a window would be pushed up and coins wrapped in newspaper flung down to the grateful performers. At other times angry voices would invite them to shut up and shove off; but as one went another came and the din was often so deafening I had to shut the window and draw the curtain before returning to my proof-reading.

But it was difficult to shut out the sounds. When the children played in the backgreen they always appeared to be threatening to kill each other. 'Ye're a deevil! I'll murder ye!' was their constant cry. But sometimes they changed their tune and called up to their home window for a 'piece' to eat. A piece of bread and jelly was what they wanted.

'Ma! MA!' they yelled at the pitch of their voices (Never 'Pa! PA!') 'Ma! I want a jelly piece. Aw! MA!' Sometimes they pleaded for so long and sounded so pathetic I was tempted to fling out a stale currant bun, but usually Ma's heart softened and a jelly-piece wrapped in a page from last night's evening paper was flung down. It was usually accompanied by some stern warnings. 'Hurry up an' come hame or your faither'll kill ye!'

Goodness knows how the children survived so many threats and on a diet of such scrappy food!

It was a wonder I survived myself. What with the lack of fresh air and exercise, and my scrimpy meals, I certainly grew paler and thinner; but I was so engrossed in my new job that I scarcely noticed my surroundings or how I was feeling. Nothing else mattered when I was working on the proofs, but now and again I came to with a start when a ball bounced against my door. The Colman children used the hallway as a playground and occasionally became obstreperous in their games. I could hear them sniffling and giggling; and now and again my door would open quietly and an inquisitive pair of eyes would gaze at me. But when I paid no attention the door was shut and I was left to my own devices.

What I dreaded most was when I heard a tap at the door and the gentlemanly man came in with a scuttle of coals to replenish my fire. Having done the deed he lingered half in half out of the doorway, hoping for some conversation. I could sense the man had little in common with his meal-ticket wife and was doubtless longing for a 'decent' talk. He kept eyeing my proofs and saying, 'I see you're busy,' hoping no doubt to trap me into a discussion about my work; but I just nodded my head and he was forced to wander away.

Yes! I *was* busy but it was a happy busyness.

There were times, of course, when I felt like a caged bird, yet this was something I had always wanted to do: to gain independence and pursue my writing career. So I struggled on with the proofs, learning some strange and unrelated titbits in the process: about the Highest Buildings in the World, Life on the Amazon, the Flora and Fauna of the USA, Famous Inventors of all Ages, Composers and their Music, and what to do in Sudden Emergencies.

Sometimes, weighed down with weariness, I sank back in my chair declaring to myself, 'I can't do it! I'll never last out the whole fortnight.'

But I did.

One morning nearing the end of my stint I was summoned to a director's room. Mr Collins, without looking directly at me, murmured that I had been very satisfactory and offered me a permanent job.

Help!

I would have to go home for the weekend to think it over and to bring back more things if I decided to accept.

# 4. Home Truths

essie was appalled when she saw me. She peered
at me through her spectacles, then over them
and cried: 'Mercy lassie! Ye look like a ghost. I
wouldn't gie tuppence for ye.'

She was angry at me, furious at Mrs Colman
for not feeding me properly, cross at 'that office'
for cooping me up. Angriest of all at the possi-
bility of my going back.

'Ye'd be as deid as a doornail in nae time,' she
prophesied dolefully. 'Whaur's your rummlegumption?' Where, indeed! *Rummlegumption*, of
course, was the commonsense Jessie had been
trying to instil in me since I was a bairn. 'Gang
oot into the fresh air an' forget aboot it.'

I went out willingly enough and gulped the
good Border air, but how could I forget about
it? Not when such an exciting future was being

dangled before my eyes. They might even raise my salary, the bosses had told me. (After a year they added cautiously.) I was already getting more than 'ordinary' female employees; but perhaps they could get round that by elevating me so that my status, if not my salary, was raised. I could be designated an assistant editor.

Fancy that!

I had been a Lady of the Manse but I thought an assistant editor a much more exalted position.

But the most pleasing prospect at the moment was a Border view.

I had run up to my crumbling castle on the hill and was sitting gazing at my favourite view, one I often saw in my mind's eye when prisoned in my Glasgow digs. *This* was my ain countree, and I could look across the frontier to that other land where the enemy used to live – the English, who were now our friends.

Nearer at hand I could see the winding road I had trudged every day on my way to the village school. I was only four and a bit when I first had to walk the two miles there and the two miles back, yet I cannot recall feeling tired or cold or hungry. It was just something I did every day.

I do remember the trouble I had when I was nearly eight and had to take Wee Maggie from the cottages to school. She was a reluctant scholar who had a habit of sitting down in the middle of the road, protesting: 'I dinna want to be lairnt!' I felt as old as ten by the time I had rounded her up like a collie dog and dragged her as far as the school gates.

I could also see the kirk to which I walked

every Sunday morning. My battered Bible was still in the family pew with despairing scribbles in the margins. 'Oh God!' 'LONG sermon!' 'Help!' A – M – E – N!!!

I had to shake myself out of my reverie when I heard the shepherd shouting, 'Watch oot! Bull's loose!'

As I had done many a time before, I jumped down from my perch, ran like the wind and scrambled over the dyke, pleased I could still put on speed in spite of having had no exercise for a fortnight. Jock shook his head at me. 'Man-lassie, it's lucky ye're still yauld,' he grunted. *Yauld* meant agile. 'How was the big toon?'

He was relieved, I think, that I had not been murdered and, like Jessie, expected me to be back home for good. I seemed to be seeing him with a fresh eye, noticing that he was leaning more heavily on his crook and that he dragged a leg as he walked off.

Everything was changing, and it was time I changed too. Time to make a life of my own. There would not always be a safe refuge for me here at home in the Borders.

Meantime I threw away my troubled thoughts, determined to enjoy this interlude before I plunged into a new life.

When I helped the current servant-lassie – Phemie – dry the dishes in the back kitchen I ventured to ask how she was getting on with Jessie.

'Her!' she sniffed, looking over her shoulder. 'She's terrible cross!'

'Och! she doesn't mean it,' I said, defending Jessie. 'Her bark's worse than her bite.'

But Phemie shook her head and said glumly, 'She barks an' bites at the same time. I'm fair fed up.'

Jessie was mumbling to herself as she swept the kitchen floor and raging at the cat for crossing her path; but I knew she would have raged at the kitchen table for want of an animate object. I think she knew at the back of her mind that I *was* going and that I might not need her guiding hand in future.

I wanted to reach out to her and say, 'Oh Jessie! Don't be downhearted! I'll never forget you no matter how old and wise I become. It was you who moulded me when I was a bairn. You'll always be part of me no matter how far I fly from the nest . . .' It was all unsaid, of course.

Bella from the post office rang up to hear about my adventures and to tell me what had happened during my absence. By the time she rang off I could not believe I had been away for only a fortnight. The minister had a boil on his neck (couldn't get his dog collar on). Mrs Brown's leg was worse. Wee Tam tore his breeks on a barbed-wire fence. Kate Scott's cousin from Galashiels had sent a postcard to say she was coming next week. 'An' wait till I tell ye aboot ma bunion . . .'

I could not think of anything as exciting in 'the office', and in any case it was difficult to get my tongue in. I tried to tell her about my digs and the Colmans; but she dismissed *them* and the

28

whole of Glasgow as rotten rubbish (she who had never been as far away as Hawick!). There was an air of 'I have spoke!' about Bella; but I enjoyed listening to her, all the same.

I had an invitation to visit Berwickshire and renew my acquaintance with my brother's parishioners. The new Lady, I heard, was doing fine, but several of my old friends wanted to see *me*. Not now, I told them. I had too much to think about. I would go later when I had solved the problem of my future.

For once I did not ask my parents' advice. I had to take a stand and make up my own mind. So I held a committee meeting with myself, leaning against a drystane dyke, and came to the most important conclusion of my life.

I must go back. I would stay in my present digs till I found better quarters. And then . . . ? The future was blurred but the decision had been made.

And having made it I took a running jump to finalize my arrangements. I blurted out my decision to Jessie without looking at her, told my parents in an off-hand way, and then began gathering my possessions together in preparation for my great exodus.

I packed an old suitcase with clothes, books and manuscripts, I ran round the farm as if saying farewell to the byre, the steading, the chicken-houses, even the pigsty, I had a last to and fro on the swing, and finally walked along the top of the garden dyke as I used to do in a fit of bravado when I was a child, showing off to myself. See me! I can do it!

Having done that, I convinced myself I would make a success of the Glasgow venture. I was longing to be free of all childhood restrictions with a chance to test my ability as a writer. If I failed it was only another rejection slip, and I had received plenty of *them* in the past. If I succeeded there was no knowing how many high dykes I could walk across without tumbling off.

Better try and fail than not try at all.

But I knew I would never completely cut the cord; and it seemed to give Jessie some consolation when she heard I would come home at frequent intervals to collect more of my belongings.

She had been thumping her chest – indigestion or indignation? – and looking so glum that I forced myself to eat large helpings of food to pacify her. Anything to counteract my feelings of guilt.

My parents did not know what to make of the move. 'Headstrong!' said Mother, shaking her own head; but Father made an imaginative gesture. In a gruff voice he told me he would order a typewriter for me to be delivered in due course to the door of my digs in Glasgow. Nothing to pay.

In due course it came! A split-new Remington portable, Good Companion, which I have in my possession to this day and which I still use when other machines are out of order. For many a year it was my only good companion, and has typed masses of scripts and books during its long lifetime. Thank you, Father.

I was too overcome to thank him properly at

the time, and of course I could never have thrown my arms round his neck and hugged him. But later on I did write him a warm letter on the new typewriter (which he ignored but I hope he read).

So that was that.

I was launched into the wide world and NOBODY could stop me from doing what I wanted.

# 5. Ready! Steady! GO!

On my first free Saturday afternoon I ventured into a large emporium in Sauchiehall Street to buy a hat.

'A red one, please!' I said firmly, before the impetus left me. I had waited long enough for this moment and I meant to savour it to the full.

The lady assistant, clad in sober black, gave me a sideways glance through her pince-nez and said pityingly: 'Red! Oh, that's not the colour this year, madam. No! Not red!'

At least she had called me madam, so I stood my ground and ignored her sensible suggestions which she was delivering in a voice like Mother's. 'What about a nice blue, or brown that would go with your colouring?'

'No!' I almost shouted it out. 'Have you not

got something brighter?' Otherwise, I implied, I'll march straight out of the shop. So there!

I thought of how Father on his periodic visits to Edinburgh would go into a fashionable shop in Princes Street and buy a hat for Mother. How had *he* done it? No doubt by charming the assistants with his gentlemanly manners, and by having the right 'eye' for what would suit Mother. For when he brought the hat home it fitted on Mother's head as if it had been specially made for her. Of course, hers had little veils and feathers, more elaborate than the one I intended to purchase.

'*Not* blue or brown!' I said, sticking to my guns, and made my way to the door.

'One moment, madam!' The lady assistant came hurrying after me. 'I think we have a purple one. Perhaps madam would like to have a look at it.'

Yes, she would. It was a cheeky wee hat and it cost all of ten shillings. Ten shillings for a purple hat to wear on my red hair! Mother would have had a fit, but it was *my* money and I was free to spend it as I liked.

'I'll just wear it,' I said while the boldness was still on me, and allowed the assistant to parcel up my old black tammy in its place. And a finicky job she made of it, too, folding and re-folding the paper, smoothing it out, snipping string with a small pair of scissors dangling from her waist, then going through the fetish of finding her pen behind her ear, inserting carbon paper in her sales book and finally summoning a lordly floor-walker to come and countersign the order. All for my purple hat!

At long last my hard-earned pound note was encased in a round wooden ball which the assistant flicked along an overhead railway to a Being who sat in a kind of cage in the centre of the shop. All I could see of *her* was her bosom as I anxiously awaited the return of my change and the receipt of my new hat.

When I went out into the street I thought everyone was staring at me but of course they weren't. I keeked in at a shop window and caught a reflected glimpse of myself. Mercy! Did the hat suit me or not? Was it too 'roary' perched on my ginger locks? I longed to ask someone who would give me a truthful opinion. I knew what Mother's verdict would have been. 'You look terrible.'

The only comment came from a pavement artist chalking in a drawing of Harry Lauder, complete with kilt and crooked stick. When he looked up and saw me he remarked, 'That hat's a bonnie colour, hen!' He did not say it suited me but I took it as a compliment and rewarded him by throwing a penny into *his* hat instead of my customary halfpenny.

One way and another it had been an expensive afternoon.

As time went by I grew accustomed to the purple hat and wore it to the office in preference to my drab tammies; but I was careful to wear *them* when I went home for the weekend and never let dab (as Jessie would have said) that I was leading a double life.

Of course, I was.

Gradually I was shedding some of my Border skin and emerging as a pseudo-Glaswegian, though it would be years before I could boast that the city belonged to me. It took me long enough to get to grips with the local lingo. It never occurred to me that *I* had an accent – a broad Border tongue laced with Jessie's sayings. I just spoke as I had always done and was surprised if someone did not understand me.

*They* had a habit of swallowing their words and a vocabulary that was new to me. What, for example, was a *jawbox*? (A kitchen sink, I was told.) So I told *them* that a *tattie-bogle* was a scarecrow; and after a time our two tongues merged.

At the office the Collins bosses, educated at Eton and Oxford, spoke with a mouthful of plum stones, so that I had to listen carefully before I could interpret their conversation, and did not always succeed. As on the day I went hither and yon searching for a shoehorn for the Chairman who had asked me to procure *something* for him. When I went back and confessed I couldn't find a shoehorn, he did not appear to want one. It was all very puzzling!

The editor had a blunt way of speaking and did not disguise his Yorkshire accent, though he never actually said 'Ee-ba-goom!' I liked listening to his homely tongue and could equate many of his sayings with Jessie's; so we all rubbed along in a kind of Tower of Babel.

Now and again a jokey man called Duncan – I was never sure if it was his first or last name – came into the office with a message. If I was alone in the room he would linger at my desk for a one-sided chat. It had to be one-sided for I never knew when he was serious or how to reply to his quips. He had a disconcerting habit of breaking into song – not any old song, always a snatch of opera. Or he would suddenly declaim a verse of poetry. 'Alas! that Spring should vanish . . .'

Oh! He *was* a strange character but I liked Duncan and his nonsense. He reminded me in a way of the Pisky Parson who used to dog my path in the days when I was a Lady of the Manse.

One day he paused at my desk and said, 'What about you and me going steady?' At least, I think that's what he said. I knew he had been a widower for many years, so perhaps he was now ready for Number Two. But I shook my head and said, 'I'm too busy.'

And so I was.

It was a different kind of busyness from that of my overcrowded life as Lady of the Manse. For the first time I was doing what I had always longed to do, spending my days in a 'literary' atmosphere in the magic world of books. In reality, I was nothing more than a dogsbody in those early days, in spite of my elevated title as assistant editor; and it was only now I realized how ignorant I was. I tried to fill the gap by watching, and listening, especially to the editor who was such a fount of knowledge I felt *he* was my university.

Meantime I earned my pennies by tackling a multiplicity of odd jobs, without any thought that I was being put upon. I just accepted as normal anything I was asked to do. For example, the man in charge of diaries – Collins Diaries were world famous – asked me one day if I knew anything about horoscopes. Not much, I told him, except that I had written a caption about the signs of the Zodiac. Well then, said he, that was a good start.

'For what?' I asked him.

Mr Blake explained that he was urgently needing extra material for his Housewife's Diary and that it would be a selling-point to include horoscopes.

'Just invent them,' he pleaded at the end of his tether. 'You could easily write a piece about each of the signs. It wouldn't take you long and I'd be very grateful.'

I don't recall if he *was* grateful but I do know it took me ages. I sweated blood over each of the signs, trying to decide what would be a fair forecast. (I have to admit I gave Pisces, my own sign, the best possible future!) And, of course, I had a great feeling of power, thinking I could control every housewife's destiny for a whole year.

When I handed my work over to Mr Blake, he took a casual glance at it and said, 'Oh! That's fine! I must think of something else you could write. Recipes, maybe . . .'

The Bumper Book man was the worst. He, poor soul, had the impossible task of making bricks without straw. Year after year he had to produce children's annuals and Big Bumper Books with the minimum of outlay. None, preferably! So how could he fill umpteen pages with stories, games, poems and pictures?

Every problem has a solution.

The trick was to go to a dreadful dump called the File Room where one could look up musty volumes from the past, and where, I was convinced, one would discover the decomposing bodies of missing directors. I was told to find and blow the dust off one of the Guard Books. These were cumbersome giants which I could scarcely lift. Inside, various items from old annuals had been pasted in with red marks at the side to indicate how often they had been re-used and in what year.

I was horrified to find that some of the stories and poems had been used half a dozen times (how short is a child's memory?) without any repayment being made to the author. The original material, complete with copyright, had been bought for a pittance, sometimes for as little as five shillings; and when I suggested it would only be fair to pay another fee, I was hushed up. The publisher had, after all, bought the copyright.

In such penny-pinching ways were publishing empires built up at the time.

Yet, in spite of such meagre recompense there was no shortage of unsolicited manuscripts arriving with every post; so many there was a backlog of months, I was told, to sort out. 'Bung them all back or throw them in the waste-basket if they haven't enclosed a stamped addressed envelope.'

My heart bled for poor Miss Moffat from Nottingham who never took no for an answer but submitted her badly typed stories week after week; or a Mr Robert Scott whose handwriting was almost indecipherable. 'I have wrote a book,' he scrawled at the foot of one of his 'pieces'. 'Would you like me to send it in?' What could I say but no?

Later on, I grew more hard-hearted though I still hated sending those awful rejection slips and longed to write an encouraging letter. 'Hard cheese! Better luck next time.'

It seemed that the Bumper Book man was always at my throat. One day he put a batch of pictures on my desk: children playing games on the seashore, on a see-saw, riding ponies, feeding their pets. 'Could you write some verses to go with these?' he asked as if it would be no bother. 'Just sign them with any name you like. They'll fill several pages of the *Tiny Tots' Annual*.'

Mine not to reason why.

I struggled long and hard over those umpty-tumpty rhymes till I became glib enough to rattle them off on almost any subject under the sun. I remember that one day I had to turn out as many as thirty non-stop to meet a deadline, after which my head was so full of rubbishy 'poetry' that when I went into a shop to make a purchase I almost spoke to the assistant in verse.

> I've got a lack
> Of thread coloured black.
> If you've got any
> I'll give you a penny.

Obeying instructions, I signed these masterpieces J. Scott, H. Brown, Mary Masters – any name that came into my head – and occasionally appended my own for variation. Years later a Collins director was amused to receive a letter from an American publisher asking, 'Is the poet Derwent still alive?' He wanted to reprint one of my verses in a children's magazine. So for a few days I felt like Longfellow and had to put up with being referred to as 'the poet Derwent'.

Now that I look back over the distance I realize there was an air of slapdashness in the firm, yet there were also rigid rules that must be obeyed, and always the threat of instant dismissal if one offended the hierarchy. For example, I remember one man being sacked out of hand ('Clear your desk and leave immediately') for inserting the wrong frontispiece in a new edition of *The Pilgrim's Progress*. Granted, he had made a foolish choice. The picture he used of the *Flying Scotsman* train was certainly the correct size. He did not bother to consider its suitability, so in *it* went and out *he* went.

There were no tribunals in those days, nor golden handshakes, only something called 'lying time', whereby one received a week's wages when leaving – and no reference if one had been sacked for misdemeanour.

So there was always a Sword of Damocles dangling overhead especially when Sir Godfrey Collins paid one of his flying visits and sacked people indiscriminately. In my early days in the firm Sir Godfrey was Secretary of State for Scotland and, like the Laird o' Cockpen, his mind was taken up 'wi' the things o' the state'. Nevertheless, he found time to pop in to the family firm when least expected, leaving a trail of blood in his wake. His word was law in the corridors of Cathedral Street as well as in Parliament, and I had been warned that if perchance he asked me a question on any subject under the sun I must be prepared to answer, for he took a dim view of dumb-bells who stammered: 'P-Please, s-sir, I d-don't know!'

I have to record that the only words I ever spoke to Sir Godfrey were 'Twelve and sixpence, sir!' This when I looked up one day to find him looming over me pointing to a page of the encyclopedia on my desk and asking in a peremptory voice: 'How much does it cost to set that page?' This was well outside my ken, but I dredged up a figure of some sort rather than sit mute. Sir Godfrey just gave me a nod before turning away, so I had no idea whether I had passed the test or not.

Nobody told me whether I was a success or a failure. They just piled more work on to me and it never occurred to me to say no. Night after night I took manuscripts home in my shabby attaché case and as soon as I had consumed Mrs Colman's tasteless meal settled down to my unpaid task. I remember receiving the odd word of thanks, but no overtime money. Certainly not from the big bosses who were scarcely aware of my existence.

Any time I met a director he was dashing along the corridor and I sidestepped to let him pass. Every member of the Collins clan appeared to be always in a tearing hurry. Sometimes I ran after one of them to pick up a paper he had dropped from the untidy sheaf he was carrying. It was said – wickedly – that he carried the same sheaf from one year's end to the other, sometimes adding to it, sometimes subtracting, often losing. Yet, in spite of such higgledy-piggledy methods, the Collins family had a good grasp of affairs inside the firm.

Outside, I was not so sure. They had been cushioned from the stings of ordinary life; accustomed to valets and butlers and never quite at ease with 'common' folk. Yet they could roll up their sleeves and toil harder than any 'worker'. They were a strange mixture, as we all are.

Each member of the ruling family was 'heid bummer' (boss) of a section defined by a letter of the alphabet: A, B, C, D, etc. His consent had to be procured before any big decision in the department could be made; and anxious heads of sections were forever seeking a rendezvous with 'my Director' to get an OK and so avoid a hold-up in their department's work.

'Have you seen Mr Ian?' they would ask breathlessly if I met one of them in the corridor. 'Which way was he going?' When I pointed, they chased after him at top speed until they were foiled when his coat-tails disappeared into a mysterious sanctum called the board-room, so sacrosanct that only a Director's secretary had the right to go and chap at the door.

Directors' secretaries lived in little cubby-holes outside their masters' rooms and were almost as powerful as the Directors themselves. Conscious of their high office, some put on hoity-toity airs; and many heads of departments sucked up to them in the hope of gaining quick access to Mr William or Mr Kenneth. So they were a cut above an ordinary secretary and were treated with great deference.

For some time I did not realize I was living in the rarified atmosphere of the Directors' corridor, and that others tiptoed quietly past the closed doors of the mighty or scuttled for safety when they heard one of the doors opening. It took me long enough to come to grips with the different sections, and to recognize the demarcation line betwixt Warehouse and Factory.

Office folk were not considered 'workers' since they never soiled their hands except with ink stains. So we were all lumped together under an umbrella called Warehouse. Factory folk were the real workers. Certainly they were the ones who made the most noise, and they were above us in more ways than one, since Factory was upstairs and Warehouse downstairs.

All day long I heard the thud of machinery overhead. It sounded deafening at first, but I grew so accustomed to it that when the machines closed down during the Fair holiday, I felt uneasy and kept cocking my ears to listen to the familiar thump-thump.

It was a case of you in your small corner and I in mine, so we kept to our own kennels and it was many months before I mastered the intricacies of the various sections.

One of my discoveries was the Counting House, ruled over by a Dickensian character called Mr Robb, an honest wee man in spite of his name. Mr Robb never sat down. He stood at a high desk with a round ruler in his hand, perpetually writing in a large ledger with a scratchy pen. He would spend hours chasing a halfpenny and not go home at night till he had found it. Above all, he hated parting with money even when told 'It's for the Chairman'; and demanded a signature before doling it out reluctantly coin by coin. There were times when Mr Robb made such a poor mouth about the firm's finances that I was almost tempted to hand him back my meagre salary. Almost!

A greater adventure was to find my way to the caseroom to make an urgent adjustment to a proof. This meant penetrating into the unknown territory in the factory and getting lost a dozen times. The fact that my mission was urgent put me in a flutter of apprehension. Would I get there in time, and should I turn right or left when I pushed open the next swing doors?

The doors led from one hive of industry to another, with machinery shuttling out sheaves of paper and piece-workers frantically collating them into neat heaps. They, the piece-workers, were women and young girls with no Music While You Work to enliven their tedious task. But the machines seemed to be singing their own tune. Hurry up! No time to lose! Keep working! Must earn a decent wage! Time is money!

They could only spare sidelong glances at me while their fingers still worked mechanically, but at least I was a diversion for them if only for a few minutes. As for where I was, I was never sure if I was in Hand-folding, Bible-sewing, Forwarding, or Marbling – all strange names to me. It was much later that they came trippingly off my tongue and that I spoke of a Father of the Chapel without batting an eyelid.

Sometimes a bosomy lady supervisor, sitting in a cubby-hole in the centre of the room, would shout: 'Are ye lost, hen?' and point me in the right direction.

The right direction led to the caseroom where Mr Davy Beavis spent his life pulling proofs and complaining about the corrections we made on them. Davy – as I got to know him – liked using long words which he did not always understand and often mispronounced. He was forever trying to 'indentify' missing proofs, and he was *never* in the wrong.

It was no use barging into the caseroom and shouting: 'Now, see here, Davy Beavis!...' He had to have egg-shell treatment.

My first encounter with Mr Beavis was over nothing more weighty than a comma. Davy had put it in where *he* thought it should be, and I had corrected it, not once but three times. Davy always corrected my correction so now I had to confront him face to face. I felt the comma was vital to my cause, but he could not see why 'God bless you merry, gentlemen' should take the place of *his* version 'God bless you, merry gentlemen.'

We had a ding-dong for a wee while, then my funny bone got the better of me, and I managed to make a joke of it. We dissolved in laughter and remained friends for all the time I was in the firm – and I was able to get my comma in the correct place.

Later on I learned how to reach the caseroom by way of a shoogly old hoist designed for portering crates of paper rather than people. As long as it kept going all was well, but if it creaked to a standstill between floors what could I do but wail for help?

It was an entirely different world to me, all so interesting that, as a willing horse, I was content to carry any additional burden no matter how heavy. It was Duncan, my 'admirer', who made me see the light.

He came into the office one day whistling a snatch of 'Madam Butterfly' and found me wearily poring over yet another extra job, writing couplets to oblige a distraught editor of children's books. Still singing, he invented new words to his tune.

> Why, why, WHY don't you say NO?
> You're the world's biggest softie!
> Say No, No, NO!
> Do your own work and nobody else's.
> Say NO! NO! NO!

I looked at him in surprise, but the truth eventually seeped through and I took his advice. Nevertheless, I felt guilt-ridden on that first free evening when I decided *not* to take any work home but to go to the pictures instead. It would make a pleasant change to gaze at Deanna Durbin on the big screen rather than at a sheaf of uncorrected proofs.

# 6. Digging In

One day I received a letter addressed to Mifs L. Derwent. It was from Jessie who still used the old *fs* for *ss*. The calligraphy reminded me of my school copybook with its terse statements: It's a long lane that has no turning. Look before you leap. Spare the rod and spoil the child.

Jessie's remarks were equally stilted. She wrote that the weather had been bad. The hens had gone off laying. Joo-anne had pains in her knee. Jock was fine but not seeing so well. She was all right but a bit slow. Maybe the time was coming when they would all have to think of retiring. Yours truly, Jessie.

'Oh don't!' I cried out to nobody in particular. 'Don't go away, Jessie! You'd leave a muckle empty hole in my heart. Wait for me. I'm coming home!'

What did a job in Glasgow matter? I mentally began packing there and then ready to take the first train back to the Borders – but it was Jessie herself who stopped me; that voice I sometimes hear even now, giving me stern and sensible advice: 'Dinna be daft, lassie. Ye've put your hand to the plough. There's no turning back.'

But I would go back at the first opportunity, if only for a weekend. Meantime I would stick to my guns and not take work home every night, apart from an occasional 'obligement'. 'I've got to make a speech at a Burns Supper and I haven't a clue what to say. I'm sure *you* could make one up for me.' (This from the Chairman who had learned his lessons at Eton and yet couldn't write his own speech! Auld Baldy-Heid at my village school would have given him his licks!)

I daresay it was flattering to be asked, but being at everyone's beck and call I was in danger of losing my own identity, whatever that might have been, and living vicariously in the shadow of others. So I had to speak sharply to myself. Come on, you! Live *your* life! Get on with your own writing!

I listened to my own advice, but I was too weary when I got home to the digs at night to puzzle my brains. So I listened instead to that Border voice of Jessie's, telling me to get ootside and stretch my legs! (That was what I needed! Fresh air and exercise.)

I did walk to work each day but this was through crowded streets and in a polluted atmosphere. It was *fresh* air I needed. I had heard Glasgow referred to as the 'dear green place', but

48

where was all this greenery? In the parks, I was told. There were dozens of them dotted in and around the city where one could walk for miles without encountering anything wilder than a squirrel or a mallard making its way back to the duckpond.

The weather was improving and the days getting lighter, so I set out at weekends to find a breath of fresh air. Soon I discovered two dear green places: the West End Park and the Botanic Gardens where I could swing my arms and stride along without fear of bumping into anyone. In some parts it was *verboten* to walk on the grass but if I could find a space where there were no forbidding notices I took to my heels and scampered like a dog let off the leash. The air was freshish rather than *really* fresh, yet the exercise made my blood tingle. My lungs were expanding and I felt I was tuning myself up. The air even whipped a little colour into my cheeks.

I had never been a stroller so I didn't dawdle but kept up a cracking pace till I had to subside, exhausted, on one of the park benches. Occasionally I encountered a keeper who called out in an amused voice: 'What's the hurry, hen? Are ye catchin' a train?'

It was in the Botanic Gardens that I first saw a Punch and Judy show and was horrified at its viciousness. But the gaping children seemed to enjoy the violence and screamed with delight every time a blow was struck. No! Not for me! I would sooner listen to Jessie's stories in the byre.

Oh Jessie! Don't give up.

Having heard of her threat to retire, it was strange that I should receive an invitation to a retirement ceremony at the office. Old Mr Crawford from Stationery was to be presented with a clock inscribed, 'For long and faithful service'.

Why a *clock*, I wondered? Mr Crawford had clocked in on time for over fifty years. Now that he was retiring, could the poor soul not be left in peace without hearing his remaining time on earth ticking away second by second? Oh no! It was the done thing to receive either a gold watch or a clock to display proudly on the mantelpiece for all to admire.

'That's my clock. Mr William himself presented it to me. See! There's my name and inscription. For long and faithful service . . .'

The sweat, the toil, the long hours, the meagre wages, the hard words – all were forgotten, soothed away by the tick-tock of a timepiece. *That* was his reward.

I stayed well in the background at Mr Crawford's ceremony. The forefront was no place for females who were there only on sufferance. In my case, I think old Mr Crawford invited me because I had lent him a listening lug in the weeks running up to his Great Day. He could talk of nothing else when he came into the office and would linger at my desk to tell me how much he was looking forward to his freedom. I wondered if he was protesting too much. He seemed to be trying to bolster himself up against the long empty days ahead. There had been no time in his life for hobbies so what could he look forward to except the ticking of his clock?

In all his working days George Crawford had never been known to utter a wrong word about his foreman. Until now! Suddenly he let loose all the exasperation he must have been bottling up for years. 'Him!' he said to me, baring his teeth like a snarling mongrel. 'I'll give *him* his character before I leave. You'll see! I can't wait to get out of the door. It'll be the happiest day of my life . . .'

But, of course, it was all bluff. I was thankful to be in the background when the ceremony began, for it was the first time I had seen a man burst into tears, and I was so embarrassed I almost followed suit.

When the hated foreman spoke about how he had depended on George for years and how they would all miss him, the old man's lip began to tremble like a baby's. And when the Chairman himself handed over the long-service clock and shook him by the hand, he broke down completely.

I did not know where to look as he brushed away his tears with the back of his hand. His wife, who had a prominent place for the first time in her life, brought out a handkerchief to wipe her own streaming eyes – and the awful moment came when George embarked on his speech. Nothing would stop him. He had a speech to make and he was going to make it. We all looked down at our toes except Mrs Crawford who mouthed every word with him.

Oh! It was terrible. I felt emotionally drained by the time it was over.

There was a polite hand-clapping, some nose-blowing – and once the bosses were out of sight a return of the belligerent mood. Lucky him! bragged Mr Crawford. *He* could have a long lie tomorrow while the poor slaves went to work. *They* would be slogging in their prison, but *he* would be free. He wouldn't miss Cathedral Street one little bit! Would anyone like another look at the inscription on his clock?

All very bold and brave! In a few days he was back at his old haunts, trying to put a swagger in his step and pretending he was having the time of his life.

Sometimes I would look up from my desk and there he was, standing with a hang-dog expression on his face, waiting hopefully for a friendly word.

'Oh hullo! How are you enjoying your retirement?'

'It's great!' said he, bluffing it out. 'There's no hurry in the morning. The wife sends me out to do the shopping.' He made a *mou* as he said it. 'Then there's the bools.' (That was the bowling.) 'And I whiles come in here to have a word with my old mates.' He sighed. 'But they're all so busy. They've no time to blether.'

He had time now, but no one to blether to. It seemed unfair, I thought. What a pity his retirement had not happened when he was young enough to enjoy it! And to hell with the ticking clock.

Watch it! I warned myself. Don't stay on too

long or *you*'ll be caught. Already I was seeing everything through Collins spectacles. When I looked in a bookshop it was to see how many of the firm's publications were on display, and when I caught sight of one I had helped to edit, I felt a glow of pride as I leafed through the pages. That comma would not have been in the correct place but for me! And *I* wrote that caption, using apt alliteration's artful aid: Mickey Mouse Makes Millions Merry. Rather good, I thought! I wonder if anyone else will notice it.

My name was not on the book but my heart and soul were in it. Seeing it in the shop was as good a reward to me as old George Crawford's clock was to him.

I kept reminding myself I had my own life to lead and my own books to write, but the struggle as usual was to find time to write – and peace. Peace! My digs were becoming increasingly noisy, not only from the din of the backgreen performers and the scuffles of the children playing in the passage outside my door, but I was becoming fed up with the nightly visits of Gentleman Joe, my landlady's husband, calling in to disturb my train of thought – and my new follower, the biggest pest of all, though she was only a bow-legged toddler.

Letty was the youngest of the Colman brood, soon to be replaced by another for her mother was expecting yet again. Letty reminded me of the school poem: 'I have a little shadow that goes in and out with me.' How to get in and out without Letty was *my* pressing problem. No matter how furtively I tiptoed, there she was ready to follow me to work each morning, and waiting on the doorstep for me when I came home at night. Oh! She *was* a nuisance!

I have to say the attraction was not mutual. There was something 'sleekit' about Letty, and a crafty look in her eyes, as if she was sizing me up, wondering how far she could go. I tried to harden my heart and shut her out of my room; but at intervals during the evening I would look up, and again there she was standing sucking her thumb, having appeared through the door like magic, waiting for me to say: 'Would you like a sweetie?' then her eyes would sparkle and her head nod vigorously. She had achieved her objective!

I was fond of sweets myself but could not always afford to buy them so there were times when I had to say, 'No, Letty! No sweeties!' At that, she would stamp her small foot angrily and close her fists as if about to strike me. Sometimes she gave me such a look I almost flinched and drew back to protect myself.

Don't be daft, I told myself, she's only a wee lassie who deserves a smacked bottom. But *I* was in no position to chastise her; and trying to get the better of Letty was becoming an obsession with me. There were times when I thought I saw the look of a calculating criminal in her eyes. And indeed it was not long before I caught her in her first thieving act.

I noticed when I arrived home one night that she was wearing a string of blue beads. They were rubbishy glass beads which I occasionally wore to brighten up an old jumper but more often left lying on my dressing-table. Tonight they were missing from their customary place and had transferred themselves to Letty's grubby little neck. She was welcome to them for they were not worth bothering about, yet I felt I could not let the incident pass without teaching her a lesson about right and wrong.

'Have you seen my blue beads, Letty?' I asked casually when she came sidling into my room later that night, hoping to mooch a sweetie. A vigorous shake of the head. She did not even finger the beads at her throat or look in the least bit guilty.

'Well, would you like to see them?' I asked, less casually this time.

Yes! the head nodded up and down. Letty would like to see the blue beads.

'Right!' I placed her in front of the dressing-table and swung down the mirror so that she could see herself. 'Look in there, Letty. Can you see the beads?'

Letty stood on tiptoe to look. When she caught sight of herself she smiled and nodded. Yes! She could see the blue beads. But was she abashed? Not a bit! She had acquired the beads and she meant to keep them. 'A thweetie?' she lisped, giving me one of her belligerent looks. The incident was over as far as Letty was concerned.

I knew I had not handled the situation in the right way. Imagine letting a wee smout like that get the better of me! What would Jessie at home have done, I wondered, and how had she kept *me* on a straight path when I was a bairn? How lucky I had been, I reminded myself, to have had someone like Jessie to guide me. Poor Letty had nobody. She was under-nourished, unloved, uncared for. Who could blame her for snatching anything she could find?

All very well! But one day when I met her wearing my new purple hat, I realized the time had come when I must make the effort to move. The Colmans and I must part.

But before I could make the move I received another letter addressed to *Mifs L. Derwent*, not in Jessie's writing this time, but in the combined fists of Joo-anne – her sister – and Jock-the-herd, her brother. When I read the contents, I did not hesitate, but caught the first train home.

# 7. Settling Down

What a cheek I had, telling Jessie one of her own stories! I would never have dared had she not been a captive audience, lying in bed looking at me through half-closed eyes.

She was the same Jessie though 'poorly'. The letter had indicated she was asking for me and, reading it, I remembered how often I had called for her when in the throes of my childhood ailments. Measles, mumps, fevers, broken bones, toothache (Oh toothache! 'the hell o' a' diseases', Burns called it, was the worst of the lot) all had been made bearable by Jessie's ministrations. I wondered if I could repay some of the comfort she had given me in the old days.

I was holding her hand but could get no response. Nevertheless, I continued with the story. It was the one about a centipede called

Meggy-mony-feet. As a child I had been intrigued by the story as Jessie told it, and could visualize Meggy with her hundred feet getting trapped in a tin of treacle. Would she ever escape? Even though I knew there would be a happy ending, I held my breath as a bairn waiting for Jessie to tell me how Meggy got out.

I had never seen Jessie in bed before. Her features against the pillow looked sharper and her nose more aquiline. A stiff plait of steel-grey hair lay outside the patchwork counterpane which was tidily tucked up to her chin. Jessie never gave way to slovenliness even when she was ill; but no wonder Jock and Joo-anne had been alarmed when she let go sufficiently to take to her bed. For once, it seemed, she had given up.

Suddenly she pursed her lips to show her mouth was dry. Joo-anne brought her a drink of water in a moustache-cup with a spout. Jessie sucked at the spout like a baby and swallowed a few mouthfuls. Then she turned her head on her pillow and fell asleep.

Jock-the-herd, sitting in his stocking-soles, swung the kettle on the swey over the fire so that we could all have a cup of tea; and Joo-anne, who stammered in times of stress, remarked: 'She'll d-d-do! She's on the m-m-mend!'

And so it proved; though I did not go back to Glasgow straight away but waited till Jessie was back on her feet. Old Dr Little, who knew her type, advised us to let Jessie follow her own instincts and do light work 'within reason'. Reasonable or not, she was on her feet next day, and the day after I was taking her for little walks in the fields surrounding the shepherd's cottage. The walks were for my benefit, I told her. It was so difficult to get a breath of really fresh air in Glasgow!

'A'weel! Ye should bide at hame!' grumped Jessie, though she knew *that* was a lost cause.

But the fact that she was grumpy was a good sign. In a day or two she was back in the farmhouse kitchen, peeling potatoes and gouging out their eyes while giving Phemie her character. 'That article' had let everything go to pigs and whistles during her absence. Look at the kitchen table! It could do with a good scrubbing; and when was the doorstep last pipe-clayed? It was high time she was back.

Oh! It was great to hear her ranting and raging. I applauded Phemie for ducking the verbal blows without answering back and unobtrusively helping the old woman by lifting heavy pails and pans. I think she was pleased to have Jessie back at the helm. No one wanted the old order to change.

Certainly I didn't.

Yet I knew I must use my return ticket and get back to my desk in Glasgow as soon as possible.

If anyone had missed me while I was away they never told me. I was immediately plunged into the work of that busy office, and caught up in the excitement of the Annual Trip.

Little did I dream the day would come when I would be wearing a paper hat with KISS ME QUICK printed on it and dancing the conga on board an old paddle steamer called the *Waverley*.

59

We – that is, every employee of the firm plus wives and children – were granted the great treat every year of sailing down the river Clyde (*Doon the Watter*, the Glaswegians called it) in company with the bosses who boarded the boat halfway, at Gourock or Greenock, to avoid the tedium of a long slow sail from the Broomielaw.

It was no tedium to me, experiencing it for the first time, bamboozled by all the sights and sounds on board, and goggle-eyed at the beautiful scenery of the Clyde. Sailing 'doon the Watter', I soon discovered, was one of the bonuses of living in Glasgow. There were so many fascinating islands dotted around the estuary: Arran, Bute, the Comrie: and *real* fresh air with a salty tang in it, even better than the Border breezes.

But it was not easy to take it all in on a Collins trip. It was difficult enough to recognize some of the workers in their Sunday garb, and to decide who was whose wife. Mercy me! Fancy the likes of *her* marrying *him*! (Or the other way round.)

They and their children were subdued at the start and some remained like that throughout the day; but others let down their hair the moment the boat backed away from the Broomielaw and the band began to play: 'We're No' Awa' To Bide Awa'.'

Great cheers rose into the air. The Trip had begun.

Children raced round the boat to let off steam, some of the grown-ups went down below for 'a wee refreshment', and the wives huddled together to exchange gossip – and sometimes little sips of sherry from bottles produced from the innermost recesses of their bosoms. Their faces took on an added glow, and excitement mounted as the boat drew in to Greenock where the high and mighty were to come on board.

The good ship was in danger of turning turtle as everyone hurried to the side to welcome the gentry up the gangway. The loudest cheer was for the Chairman – 'Good old Billy!' – from those who would never have dared address him so familiarly in normal circumstances. He gave them all a wan smile and they scuttled away and kept out of his reach for the rest of the day. To give him credit the Chairman, along with his party, did his best to mingle and greet as many workers as he managed to recognize.

In later years when *I* came on board with the bosses, Good old Billy used to fire agonized questions at me from the corner of his mouth. 'Quick! Tell me who's that coming forward? Is it Ainslie or Harris?' 'Stoddart!' I would whisper just in time for him to hold out his hand. 'Oh hullo, Stoddart! A great day for the Trip!'

'Yessir!'

Another loyal employee satisfied!

On that first trip I could not have told a Stoddart from a Wotherspoon, and I doubt if anyone knew who *I* was. I hardly knew myself. My KISS ME QUICK hat fell off before anyone took up the challenge, and my arms were almost tugged out of their sockets by enthusiastic conga-ers who tried to pull me from the sharp end to the blunt, round funnels, over shipboard obstacles and almost over the side into the Clyde.

Sometimes the band played 'pretty' tunes like the 'Bluebell Waltz' so that Mr and Mrs Thing could get up together and waltz round the deck. For the more sprightly we had an Eightsome Reel with dozens of extras joining in and everyone hooching like mad even, it seemed, the seagulls swirling overhead.

On that first trip we sailed to an unpronounceable destination – Tighnabruaich – and spilled out to stretch our legs in a grassy field where the Sports were to be held. But first we had to be fed. This was done by the simple process of handing out 'pokes' (paper bags) filled with sausage rolls, 'fly cemeteries', shortbread, coffee buns and, if we were lucky, a chocolate biscuit. This was all washed down by lemonade for the youngsters and tea for the grown-ups, made by Mr Robb from the Counting House who had travelled in advance to set up a giant urn and have the brew properly stewed by the time we arrived.

In later years when we were elevated to a bigger ship – *Queen Mary II* – we had proper lunches on board, or were entertained when we sailed to Dunoon by the Lord Provost who awaited our arrival at the pier, wearing his robes and chains.

But at Tighnabruaich the trippers were happy enough to swap the contents of their paper pokes – a sausage roll for a chocolate biscuit – and to blow up the bags and burst them when they were empty. There was a sweetie-scramble for the children – a great scattering of liquorice allsorts and dolly mixtures – then a quick tidy-up under Mr Robb's eagle eye before we were ready for the races.

The men rolled up their trouser-legs and ran in their stocking-soles, taking a tumble now and again on the uneven ground before puffing to the tape to claim their winnings. One shilling for first, sixpence for second, reluctantly handed over by Mr Robb. The children were all rewarded with pennies whether they won or not; and the older lads risked life and limb by falling off their perches during a strenuous pillow-fight.

The greatest treat of all was when the bosses joined in and behaved like ordinary human beings. The Collins clan were all great sports (in more ways than one) – many of them were *Blues* – and did not mind looking ridiculous in front of their work force. A great cheer rose up when Good old Billy grabbed one of the pillows and began to belabour Mr Thingummy from Accounts till he fell wounded to the ground.

We noticed there was a hole in the Chairman's sock and that his galluses (braces) were fastened with safety-pins. Somehow it made him more likeable. 'Hooray! Good old Billy!'

Some of the younger lads and lasses wandered towards a nearby hill and disappeared amongst the bracken and overgrown ferns. When it was time to leave and after the vigilantes had done their clearing up, the *Waverley* sounded the first *toot* to warn stragglers to come on board. The second was a louder *toot-toot* and the third a peremptory *toot-toot-TOOT!*

'That's it! They can walk hame!' grunted Mr Robb, helping to lug the tea-urn up the gangway. But he was not as hard-hearted as he sounded. If he heard distressed shrieks and saw breathless couples emerging from the greenery to stumble down the hill, he gave orders to lower the gangway and stood waiting, watch in hand, till the blushing culprits hurried on board. Once, it was said, Good old Billy himself went for a climb to the top of the hill and came lollopping down at the last minute to take a great leap on board without waiting for the gangway.

It was a true saying about Collins Trips that there was always an ambulance waiting at the quayside when the boat arrived back in Glasgow, ready to take a wounded warrior to the Royal Infirmary. If it was not a small boy who had broken his nose by tumbling over the big drum, it was a lassie whose thumb was trapped in a lemonade bottle and who was wailing blue murder. Or it might be an inebriated gent who wanted to fight everyone in sight. 'Come on, Jimmy! Stick 'em up— I'll show ye!'

But it was all a sign that a good time had been enjoyed by all. At the end we raised another cheer though we had no idea what we were cheering for, and dispersed at the Broomielaw to wander wearily to our separate homes.

The Trip was over for another year.

It was a gradual process, mastering the intricacies of the firm. As it was the only one I had worked for I had no idea if it was special, or if the same applied to Blackie, for example, our friendly rivals across the way. Or were they friendly? We were inclined to look down our noses at them. Didn't it take them a whole week to put in a comma and another week to delete it? Be that as it may, they did a roaring trade in Bumpers. Did they pay as little for the contents and re-use them as often as we did? I expect so! Anyway, we avoided meeting the Blackie directors face to face if our paths crossed when walking along Cathedral Street; though I think the big bosses got together now and then on common ground. And, indeed, later on 'we' bought part of their factory across the way; but even though it belonged to 'us' it was still referred to as Blackie's building.

Oh! It was not easy for me to fathom it all out. There were so many different things to learn apart from my work at the desk.

For example, it took me ages to understand the etiquette of 'going round with a sheet'. It appeared that when someone in a department was about to leave to get married, one of her friends set off with a long sheet of paper to collect for a going-away present. To begin with, I was completely baffled. 'It's Jeannie Scott,' the collector would say, waving the sheet in front of me. 'Are ye putting your name doon?' Even though I had never met Jeannie Scott, I found myself meekly agreeing to contribute sixpence or a shilling to her present.

I always hoped they would return the compliment when I married a millionaire, but, as I reminded myself sadly: 'They'd a' be deid by then.'

It was a strange business. Stranger still the

sending-off of a bride-to-be after her buddies had gone round with the sheet. On her last day at work her desk, or her cubby-hole in the factory, would be bedecked with strange objects and a 'witty' verse hung up for all to read.

> Mary Macfarlane's getting wed.
> Mary Macfarlane's going to bed.
> And here's her po.
> Her po-po-PO
> To put below
> Mary Macfarlane's bed.

There was no escape for Mary Macfarlane, not that she tried to get away from her tormentors. She expected a 'doing' and she got it. The chamber-pot had pride of place, filled with useful household gadgets: dusters, small brushes, scouring soap, bathbrick, and various other cleaning materials. The willing victim was robed in an old curtain with a mock train and a 'veil' on her head; and now she was ready to be marched off home with her followers beating a tin tray and rattling the chamber-pot to attract attention so that all the passers-by could pat the bride on her back till the poor lassie must have been black and blue, though she appeared to like it.

Where was the groom? I don't remember ever seeing *him*. But I do remember that those who contributed to the sending-off eventually reaped their reward, for some weeks later round came the sheet again brought by the collector who ticked off my name before handing me a thank-you offering from the bride – now gone for ever from my ken – and as I recall it was always a bar of chocolate. So while the new bride settled in to her single-end, I sat at my desk and comforted myself by sucking my consolation present.

# 8.  Finding My Feet Again

I was becoming accustomed to asking for directions and finding helpful Glaswegians willing to go the other mile to show me the way. Sometimes it was difficult to shake them off and avoid answering their friendly questions.

'Is't a single end, hen?' the man was asking me as he showed me the way to Parnie Street. I had been bidden there to partake of a celebration tea to mark Jeannie Young's retiral after sixty-five years of unblemished service. Sixty-five years with the one firm and never off ill!

I had no idea what a single-end was, but suddenly I knew I was nearing my destination when I heard Harry Lauder singing at the pitch of his voice. Jeannie had told me one of the gifts she had received from the bosses was a gramophone, and she was obviously determined the entire neighbourhood should hear it going at full blast.

'It's here, thank you,' I told my escort. He had cocked his head to listen to the music and evidently understood my mission.

'Up that close, hen!' he said, pointing to a nearby tenement. 'That's where Jeannie Young bides.'

As I walked up the worn stone steps the music grew louder, reminding me of the days when I used to crank up the old gramophone at the farmhouse; though our old records had been played so often that Harry Lauder could never have sung all the way through without stopping at the 'scratchy bits'.

'D'ye like it?' shouted Jeannie from the open door of her one-roomed flat. Her single-end.

'Yes!' I yelled back; and thereafter gave up the struggle to make myself heard above the din. Jeannie had invited half a dozen of her cronies from the factory, all accustomed to bawling above the noise of machinery, so, while *they* shouted to each other *I* just watched and listened.

Jeannie and I had become friendly when I encountered her on my occasional jaunts to the factory. One day she rescued me when I was taking the wrong turning, and gradually tucked me under her wing like a mother hen. I think she was pleased to have a friend from the warehouse, especially one from the Directors' corridor who was young enough to hang on her words as she told tales of the old days in Collins. She knew every single thing about everybody, and used to dig me in the ribs, saying; 'I could spill the beans, hen!' But she was too loyal to do that.

The other 'girls', all in their sixties and all heads of their sections in the factory, were admiring Jeannie's presents: the clock, the gramophone, the handbag. Best of all the cheque handed over by the Chairman himself.

'What did he say, Jeannie?'

'When he shook hands wi' me?' That was the great thing, that he had shaken hands with her. 'He said: "Well done, Jeannie. Well done." '

'Mercy!' said the others, impressed. 'Did he call ye Jeannie, Jeannie?'

'Uhuh.' Jeannie tried to imitate the Chairman's voice. ' "Well done, Jeannie. Well done . . . " '

The waves of talk washed over me as I gazed around Jeannie's compact kitchen-living-room, at the vase of artificial flowers on the windowsill, the china dogs on the mantelpiece, at the old organ, handed down no doubt from one of her ancestors with the sewing machine (Singer) sitting on top of it, at the jawbox, and the box bed she let down from the wall every night, the creepie stool where her cat lay snoring and at the photographs which crowded every cranny.

The pictures were all of the Collins clan, some real photographs, others extracted from news-papers; of weddings, christenings, visits to garden parties, even Buckingham Palace. The people in the pictures were 'family' to Jeannie and she never tired of talking about them.

We were squashed like sardines round the table, with a three-tiered cake stand in the centre and knives and forks set at each place for a high tea. Cold ham and tomato on a bed of lettuce with brown sauce to be plastered over the meat, and thick slices of bread already buttered.

'More sugar, hen?'

'No, no! *Less*, please!'

But Jeannie gave me more, out of the generosity of her heart.

The fire was so hot and the talk so loud that I had to keep a grip of myself not to faint. Watch it! Don't spoil their fun!

They were talking, of course, about the Collins family, living through them a second life. Vicariously, they went on hunting trips, holidayed in the South of France, skied, visited Australia, were divorced, had miscarriages, gave birth, were unfaithful, and knighted by the monarch. Oh! The rich lives that were led in Parnie Street – and not a self-pitying sigh or a murmur of envy.

I could not but admire Jeannie. No lad had come along to claim her hand in marriage, she had no relatives to help her, so she was forced to fend for herself. Over the years, by doing piece-work and eventually being made head of her section, she had amassed a competence, enough to pay the rent of her single-end and put by a few pennies for a rainy day. Particularly a penny a week 'burial money' so that there would be no pauper's grave for her.

Oh! Well done, Jeannie!

I hoped she might have a flutter with the Chairman's cheque. The 'girls' were urging her to buy a new costume but this was too big a decision to take without months of plotting and planning. 'What d'ye think o' ma wee hoose?' she asked me as I was leaving.

'It's cosy,' I told her truthfully, and went quickly down the stone steps to gulp some fresh air in the street. I walked away at twice my usual pace as if escaping from a trap. Never, never, NEVER I kept telling myself. Remember you have a life of your own to lead . . .

All the same, 'Well done, Jeannie!'

At that time women's lib. had not been invented, so it was the men who were the most important members of the firm, though I suspected its prosperity owed much to the cheap labour of the factory girls. Yet the men themselves were not entirely safe. As the end of the year drew nigh it was noticeable there was a distinct uneasiness in the male fraternity prior to the dreaded Annual Meetings.

While not exactly cooking the books the heads of departments were busy adding and subtracting figures in their ledgers in a way that would have appalled Mr Robb if he had found out. Anything to make their results look better. 'He'll maybe not ask to see the figures,' was their hope as they waited their turn to be interviewed outside the board-room door.

Each head of department was summoned individually to learn his fate. Some had hang-dog looks when they went in and jaunty steps when they emerged to boast of a bonus or an increase in salary; but it could be the other way round and they could come out with slouched shoulders looking as if they had been horsewhipped.

There was a stir of strange men about the place

as the reps. foregathered for the annual meetings from 'a' the airts', folk whose names I had heard but whose faces were a blank to me. So *that*'s Mr Jones, I thought! Goodness! I never imagined him with a wee moustache. And Peter McRory's twice the size I pictured him. Some were nicer and others nastier than they had appeared from their letters. There was a jokey one, of course, ready to dig me in the ribs and mutter innuendos with double meanings. 'I've no idea what you're talking about,' I told him cuttingly.

Having survived their interviews the next hurdle was the Dinner, an all-male event which remained a mystery to me for years. It was held in the city's largest hotel, attended by all the bosses, heads of departments, hand-picked reps., and a few favoured factory managers. Not a skirt in sight. Even the baked Alaska was brought to the tables by male servitors looking like tailors' dummies.

A difficult situation arose in later years when the Chairman requested a song during the interval, and suggested his favourite ditty, 'Cherry Ripe'. A lady singer had to be recruited for the purpose and was kept discreetly hidden in the background, and whisked away after her mission was accomplished. It was 'Cherry Ripe' or nothing; so the company got 'Cherry Ripe'!

The man who suffered most on such occasions was the unfortunate gent who had been detailed to propose a toast to the firm. It was, of course, an honour to be picked from the ruck and seated beside the mighty during the preceding meal; but what a waste of food! How could he enjoy a spoonful of cockie-leekie soup or a bite of roast beef with such a fate hanging over his head? Even the bread rolls were crumbled to nothing in nerveless fingers.

It was a different matter next day when he could brag to his pals who had not been invited to the Dinner. 'Yes! I was sitting next the Chairman, and I said to him . . .' The post-dinner pleasure was almost worth the pre-speech pain.

Later on, I became involved in the Dinner myself in a roundabout way when one of the speakers begged me for a few *bon mots* to liven up his 'piece'. But it was difficult to lure speakers away from the rigid pattern of likening the firm to a good ship being navigated through stormy seas by the Chairman at the helm who steered it into calm channels (applause!).

Sink that ship, I suggested. Make a short snappy speech with a few home truths and a few good jokes. And DON'T BE BORING!

'All very well for you,' I was told. 'You'll not be there.'

Yes, I will, in spirit! And perhaps the day will come when *females* will be on the board and sit at the high table. So there!

Don't talk rubbish was the answer to *that*!

All the same, they accepted some of my light-hearted offerings, as well as the applause with which the speech was greeted. Females could be tolerated, I found, as long as they kept their place; but a man was a man, for a' that!

The London males, lofty members of the firm who inhabited splendid premises in St James's

Place – a mansion rather than an office – attended the Dinner, and in the absence of an interpreter had no notion what the Scots were saying. 'And vicey-versy,' said one of our wags!

Various visiting dignitaries were also invited to break bread at the annual feast. I remember catching a passing glimpse of a great man called Dr Giovanni Mardersteig who had come from Verona to devise a new typeface for the firm. He called it *Fontana* and Eric Gill fashioned the firm's logo which is in use to this day. Later on, when I helped to run the house magazine called Fontana, I became (incognito, I hoped) the firm's cat, *Fontanella*, who wrote silly poems and used her sharp claws to take digs at the directors.

I was still being asked to take on odd jobs, one of them correcting apprentices' exam papers. The young lads – all slow readers and writers – were given a questionnaire, simple enough on the surface but evidently too difficult for them.

*Question.* What is the distance between Glasgow and Edinburgh?
*Answer.* I dinna ken.
*Question.* What would you do if you were the Lord Provost?
*Answer.* Nothing.
*Question.* How do you fill your leisure hours?
*Answer.* Never have none.

It was all so stilted that I asked if I could set a new paper, and when I was told to go ahead tried to devise subjects that might be nearer the young lads' hearts. Football, for example. Having been brought up on rugby, soccer was a mystery to me at that time; but one could not

75

live long in Glasgow without hearing about the giant teams: Rangers and Celtic.

So I set some simple questions about football which seemed to appeal more to the apprentices. At least, they had plenty to say, often covering page after page, though I have to admit their spelling did not improve – but at least *I* learned a great deal about the game!

As for the bosses they were not sure whether to praise or blame me, so they did neither.

# 9. Leisure And Pleasure

I was still a country mouse at heart, unaccustomed to crowds and stepping off the pavement to let others pass; but I was enjoying having a taste of freedom for the first time in my life; and if I was to become a town mouse I might as well take advantage of the amenities Glasgow had to offer.

And it had plenty.

At first, it was the talking pictures that took up my attention. Glasgow had a plethora of picture palaces with proud-looking major-domos parading up and down at the doorways, showing off their splendid uniforms. I expected them to talk in strange foreign tongues, they looked so mysterious, but all they shouted was, 'Move up, hen!' to a slowcoach in the queue.

Once inside, cushioned on a red plush seat in

the darkness, it was easy to suspend belief and escape from foggy Glasgow to sunny Hollywood where the beautiful people lived. They were all perfect. Not a blemish or a blackhead to be seen, no wrinkles on their smooth faces, not a hair out of place, and with teeth whiter than white. No wonder they smiled so often.

How I envied them as I sat in the darkness sucking a butterscotch toffee. They all lived in spacious apartments with deferential servants anticipating their every whim. They never opened a door or carried a parcel. Large limousines drew up at the exact moment, with chauffeurs touching their caps, and everyone looking immaculate. How lucky I was to share their glamorous lives for only one and ninepence.

Yet there were times when the scales fell from my eyes and I got tired of the beautiful people who never did a hand's turn from morning till night, except fall in love with gents looking like tailors' dummies. 'Away and work!' I almost shouted in the darkness (using the good old Glasgow phrase for malingerers). But what could they have worked at, these delicate damsels who would not have recognized a kitchen sink if they saw one? *They* were not made of blood and guts, like Jeannie Young of Parnie Street.

Nevertheless I got my money's worth and sat through everything till THE END was flashed on the screen. I even listened intently to 'the man with the mighty organ' when he appeared like a mushroom from below the ground, playing rippling music with his hands and feet. He wore a fancy evening dress with coat-tails swinging over the music-seat and spoke to us through a little microphone, promising to play our favourite tunes, and he did, transporting us from the Bonnie Banks o' Loch Lomond to the Lakes of Killarney.

Meantime, attendants passed quietly down the darkened aisles, shining their flashlights on the goods they had to sell. Little tubs of ice cream, chocolate bars, and toffee. We chewed quietly and tried not to rustle the sweetie papers for fear of disturbing the music-man before he disappeared down below still playing bravely till the earth closed over his head, and the next item came on.

It might be a travelogue followed by a slapstick comedy. Or Mickey Mouse. He was a great favourite with all ages, and we all cheered his exploits; but silence fell on the cinema when the big picture came on. No one moved a muscle or dreamt of sneaking out before the final chaste embrace.

Even then, we did not hurry away, but rose and stood patiently while the National Anthem was played all the way through with pictures of the Royal Family flung on the screen. Only when they had faded did we fasten up our coats before emerging into the wet streets. Such was the magic of those early talking pictures and I walked all the way back to my digs without noticing the puddles, convinced I was as beautiful as Kay Francis or even Greta Garbo.

I was fascinated to find that in one of those picture palaces people could sit at little side tables and partake of afternoon tea (maybe high tea, too) while watching Don Ameche making love to his leading lady. Town folk certainly knew how to lead sophisticated lives.

When I first came to Glasgow I could not indulge too often in such delights, having to be careful with my pennies as well as my sixpences and shillings; so though not an addict of music-hall entertainment, I ventured now and again into the Empire Theatre when I discovered that ninepence could procure a good seat.

This was a different world from the sedate picture-houses. It was an eye-opener for me to be surrounded by such a vocal audience, sometimes clapping appreciatively, at other times booing or cat-calling; and there were even times when I had to duck my head if a missile flew through the air in the direction of the stage.

I tried to applaud every act, however feeble. Poor things! They were only paid a pittance, yet they smiled bravely even when being booed. Meantime a little light flashed a number at the side of the stage to indicate what turn was coming next. Certainly there were some rubbishy acts leading up to the top of the bill who might be a stout lady called Tessie O'Shea or a 'Chocolate-Coloured Coon' who sang *She's My Lady Love*. I remember a fat gent who played the xylophone and another who set my teeth on edge by producing squeaky music on the saw.

There were trapeze artists, jugglers, mind readers, and double acts of the 'I say, I say' variety. Indeed, it was variety at its best, I suppose, and I was fortunate to have had a taste of it.

But I soon abandoned the music hall when I discovered the real theatre. At first I patronized the little theatres where actors and actresses were trying out their wings, prior to the birth of the Citizens' Theatre in which James Bridie played such an important role. In these small theatres there was limited space not only for the audience but also for the actors who could not avoid 'bumping into the furniture' on the stage, let alone each other. Yet their acting was excellent and I sat through many a great performance, shutting my eyes to the quick changes visible from the side and my ears to the occasional loud prompting. When I ventured to the 'real' theatre the names were bigger but the acting no better.

Here I could see beautiful people in the flesh, the ladies attired in lovely Parisian gowns with never a crease or a safety-pin to be seen. They moved gracefully about the stage after coming down some steps from a sunlit garden to ring for the parlourmaid who brought in afternoon tea complete with sugar tongs. The ladies deftly manipulated the sugar tongs, sipped their tea without slopping a drop into the saucer, and nibbled little sandwiches without a visible chew.

Meantime their male counterparts followed them in from the garden, wearing impeccably white trousers and twirling their boaters in their hands. They called the ladies *dahling* and looked so gallant with their neat wee moustaches, I would have liked replicas of them for my mantelpiece at home.

The actors were not the only ones drinking tea. During the interval, while male members of the audience sloped off to the bars, their ladies were handed little teatrays ordered in advance, containing all the appurtenances – apart from tongs – for a refreshing interlude. We sat primly in our places trying to eat the biscuits as daintily as the beautiful people on the stage, and not to rattle the teaspoons if the attendants had not collected the empty trays before the curtain went up. What with the men returning late to their seats and the teatrays jangling, the beginning of the next act was always a dead loss. There were whispered 'hushes' from all sides while the performers tried not to look annoyed. Guilty or not, we felt in their black books and bowed our heads in shame, fearing their wrath. Indeed, some actors powerful enough to demand perfect silence, stopped the show and stood glaring at the audience till everyone had settled down.

The biggest names in the business came to Scotland in those far-off days when plays were given a trial run in the provinces prior to their London opening. So we had the privilege of seeing the mighty before our very eyes, and gazed reverently at such actors as Noel Coward, Ralph Richardson and John Gielgud. And we enjoyed musicals with Ivor Novello, Binnie Hale, Evelyn Laye and Jessie Matthews.

I had to ration my time as well as money; yet over the years I sampled everything from Shakespeare to the 'Oh Calamity' farces. Indeed, at that time, the popularity of live entertainment was such I used to wonder if anyone stayed at home at nights, especially when Christmas approached and the pantomime season started.

Glaswegians were – and still are – pantomaniacs. The season lasted longer and longer every year, starting well before Christmas and running over the New Year for several months. No Christmas was complete without a night out at the panto: and a long night it was. As midnight approached bus drivers could be seen waiting wearily beside their coaches outside the Alhambra, the King's, the Pavilion, the Royal and other theatres ready to convey their customers home to Hamilton, Kirkintilloch, East Kilbride and many another outlying area.

These theatres were all noted for their lavish productions of the traditional favourites: *Jack and the Beanstalk, Cinderella, Mother Goose* and *Robinson Crusoe*; and each vied with the other to produce bigger and better transformation scenes. The audience, too, were transformed when they saw six white ponies come prancing on to the stage drawing a golden coach to take Cinders to the ball. Where were her tags and tatters, her mops and dusters? She was now wearing a beautiful ballgown with a diamond tiara on her head and sparkling rings on every finger, with tiny glass slippers on her feet.

Well done, Cinderella! You have transformed our own drab lives. Yes! Some day we *would* marry our prince.

But the real stars of the pantomine were the comics. *They* were the ones who drew the crowds: Will Fyffe, Tommy Morgan, Lex McLean, Duncan Macrae – rumbustious characters whose earthy humour captivated their audiences who burst into gales of laughter the moment they appeared on stage. They were usually dressed as women in ridiculous outfits – striped bloomers, crazy headgear, high-heeled shoes – and carrying shopping-baskets containing unlikely 'messages' which set them off on their local patter, much of which was ad lib. There was a great deal of good-humoured banter between stage and audience, and woe betide anyone caught in the cross-fire. The unfortunate occupants of the stage boxes (some of the boxes were almost *on* the stage) had to be ready with some repartee if they became victims of Mother Goose's 'witty' remarks.

For the more agile, Glasgow provided ample exercise on the dance floor. It was the era of the *jigging* (the local name for dancing) and the natives of Glasgow had a worldwide reputation for being 'nifty hoofers'. They served their apprenticeship at a large dance hall called the Barrows – the *Barras* in local parlance – where strong-muscled chuckers-out kept the throng under control. Here, there was no such nonsense as etiquette when requesting a damsel to dance. The fella just grabbed a partner without even a 'How about it?' and abandoned her in the middle of the floor at the end of the dance.

Even so, romance seemed to flourish, for many married couples when asked where they met, invariably replied: 'At the jiggin'.'

At the other end of the scale was the Plaza where 'respectable' people went for a night's dancing and which was a favourite venue for coming-of-age parties. These were called Twenty-firsts. 'Where are you holding your Twenty-first?'! The answer was usually, 'At the Plaza.' The company danced round the flower-decked fountain in the centre of the floor, then the lights were lowered and the band struck up: 'Twenty-one Today!' Drinks were handed round, the cake cut, and restrained kisses given and taken all round.

As far as I can recall, there were only soft drinks apart from something called a wine-cup, a heady concoction which was ladled into the glasses and which made the young girls giggle. Or maybe it was only the combination of music, emotion, and their partners looking so 'nice' in their tails and white gloves. Everything on such occasions was *nice*.

But it was all to end shortly with a big explosion called THE WAR. The simpering misses as well as their well-groomed escorts would soon be in uniform and there would be no doors for their Twenty-first keys to open.

# 10.  The Literary Scene

Never mind the drudgery, it was wonderful to be in the world of books.

The very smell of them, hot from the press, excited me as if I had taken a pep pill. I always felt keyed-up when turning over the pages. Even the old and tattered ones in the file-room had this effect, and though I sometimes wondered if familiarity would breed contempt, it never did.

Was everyone who worked in the firm bitten by the same bug? Certainly they talked incessantly about books: sales, publicity, accountancy, binding, sewing, forwarding, and all the rest; but seldom mentioned what was inside the books. Perhaps if they had been promoting *boots* instead of books they would have shown the same enthusiasm for shoelaces, slippers, brogues and goloshes.

True, some of the reps. took a quick look inside the goods they had to sell to ascertain the number of pages and to see if the books were illustrated. That seemed to suffice. And heads of departments seemed interested only in their own brand of merchandise, ignoring fiction, bibles and diaries if their particular niche was children's books; forgetting what was dinned into them every year at the annual dinner that they were all cogs in one big wheel.

The biggest cogs of all, the Directors, lived and breathed books, but did they ever *read* them? First thing the Chairman did when he arrived by train from London was to take a quick look at the bookstall in Central Station. 'Where are *our* books?' he would ask indignantly if they were not instantly visible. The unfortunate minion who had been sent to meet the train would have to rearrange the display on the bookstall so that Collins' books were uppermost. Meanwhile the Chairman was picking up rival books and manhandling them to discover their binding and other features before tossing them back on the stall where they would doubtless be unsaleable.

The divine rights of the Collins clan!

Of course, many of the stories were apocryphal and I was not sure what to believe unless I heard them from the horse's mouth. One horse told me how he had often been the victim of the late Chairman's peccadilloes, particularly of his dislike of travelling alone. When the great man had to go to London by train he commandeered someone to keep him company on the journey and turfed him out at Crewe if he was fed up with him by that time, leaving the poor man high and dry to find his way home.

This often happened, my informant told me, on a Saturday afternoon when he – the victim – had appeared in the office that morning dressed in plus-fours and hoping for a round of golf when he was free in the afternoon. The ensuing conversation when he was called to the Presence went like this:

> *Chairman* (looking over his spectacles at his victim): Going golfing, Mr Er . . . er . . . ?
> (According to my 'horse' this particular boss had a disconcerting habit of er . . . er . . . ing his victims rather than naming them.)
> *Victim:* Yessir, I was hoping . . .
> *Chairman:* And I'm hoping, Mr Er . . . er . . . that we'll go over your department's books together in the train. It leaves at one o'clock sharp . . .

There were no protests, not even a chance to telephone the wife who, however, understood what had happened to her missing husband. ('Selfish old bugger!' the 'horse' said to me, now that his tormentor was safely dead and buried.)

A later Chairman – Good old Billy – had a flair for finding a best seller, whether he read a book or not, and would travel halfway round the world in search of one. For example *Born Free,* about Elsa the lioness. These journeys always had dual purposes. Billy visited all the outposts of his empire, and caused a great stirring up when the cry was heard: 'The Chairman's coming!'

Wives redecorated their houses and were repermed in preparation. Husbands shook off their lethargy, tidied up the office and alerted local booksellers to appear with sheaves of orders in their fists. A private dinner party was laid on to which prominent members of the community were invited. Later on, when he was back home, the Chairman would say: 'I don't know how they do it in Kuala Lumpur (or Santa Barbara) but the Collins name is really well known there. I have to congratulate Mr Stevens and Mr Smith on working so hard. And I think *I've* found another best seller . . .'

For all I knew they – the Directors – may have been authors *manqué* themselves, though I doubted it, having seen some of the painfully written reports of their safaris.

Sometimes in a fit of rebellion I had a consultation with myself and decided I must branch out on my own though I was happy enough going round and round in Collins' whirlpool. I was meeting many writers on paper but none in real life. I wondered if any existed in Glasgow and how I could get in touch with them. More important, would they want to know *me*?

I had contacted a highly esteemed lady at the BBC called Kathleen Garscadden. 'Auntie Kathleen' was in charge of Children's Hour and was such a formidable character with the power of saying 'Yes' or 'No' that everyone kowtowed to her. Looking back, I can see her likeness to Jessie with the same ideas of right and wrong – black and white with no shades in between and an absolute certainty that *She Was Right*. And often she was.

Kathleen did not drink, smoke, dab powder on her nose, or flutter her lashes at a member of the opposite sex, but went home to her aged mother every night as pure as when she left home in the morning. Unto this day, Kathleen, a youthful 90-year-old, and I remain good friends and I'm always grateful to her for giving me such a good start in broadcasting and helping to bring Tammy Troot to life.

Payment was still paltry but anything extra was a welcome addition to my meagre salary, and helped to pay for such extravagances as red hats! Later on, though it could not be said to advance by leaps and bounds, the payment at least *crawled* up until I began to accumulate a little nest-egg in the bank. My 'leaving Collins' account.

It was not Kathleen's fault that the payments were so small. The BBC under Lord Reith kept such a tight hold on the purse strings that the habit was difficult to break and employees hesitated before requisitioning even a new pencil. Yet, in spite of such restrictions, Auntie Kathleen in her day was a power in the land and will always inhabit a special niche in the annals of broadcasting, along with Uncle Mac (Derek McCulloch) who operated from London.

For many years Kathleen's was the best-known voice in Scotland, eagerly listened to in cot and castle. She provided wholesome entertainment for myriads of young listeners – for old ones, too – and gave a helping hand to many beginners like myself who had good reason to be grateful to her.

It was through the BBC that my literary horizon expanded. Letters from listeners began to arrive, one inviting me to join a Writers' Club. A club for real writers! When I went along one night to view and be viewed in a rented room in Bath Street, I found a small group perusing the minutes of the last meeting, after which they went on to discuss each other's manuscripts. They had a proper constitution, I discovered, and rigid rules which they were careful to follow. They signed their names on entry, paid one shilling each to cover the rent of the room, and later another sixpence for a cup of tea. 'Bring your own buns,' I was told.

I showed them some of my printed pieces which they seemed to like – and I was in! With a membership card, number fifty-two. I think I paid half-a-crown there and then for the privilege. It was all quite painless.

I was surprised that they treated me as a *find* as well as a friend, but I had to make it quite plain from the beginning that though I worked in a publishing house I had no power to get their material published. I helped them all I could – as they helped me – to find new outlets for our work. They talked endlessly about 'markets' to which they could send their articles, poems, and short stories; and at that time there were many more openings for freelance writers.

In Glasgow alone there were two if not three evening papers, a weekly called the *Weekly Herald*, a daily paper called the *Glasgow Herald* and its little sister, the *Bulletin*. 'Have a bash at the *Bulletin*,' was the Club's suggestion; so we all bashed away at its portals and were as proud as punch when they occasionally opened to accept a piece called a *Little Bulletin*.

The pay was only ten shillings and sixpence, but the subject could be about anything under the sun so it gave us scope to try out our writing skills, and we had the pleasure of seeing our initials in print.

And so we swapped buns and market information. I was introduced to many Scottish publications: the *People's Journal*, the *People's Friend* (where Annie S. Swan held sway), the *Scots Magazine*, the *Scottish Field, Chambers' Journal* and *Maga – Blackwoods' Magazine*, where George Eliot first found an outlet for *her* stories.

We took rejection slips in our stride and were not unduly disheartened when our manuscripts were returned; but there was great rejoicing on all sides when an acceptance was announced. We were getting somewhere! The success seemed to rub off on everybody and dog-eared manuscripts were looked out to be sent off on yet another hopeful journey.

The members were all trying out their wings. Some, I suspected, would never flap them higher than the ceiling of that friendly room in Bath Street, and were content with the companionship and sticky buns. Others were more determined to make a go of it and some did indeed become regular contributors to one or other of the periodicals, or even took the plunge and wrote a book.

A book.

I sensed this was what I must do – write a book – if I was ever to get out of my rut. Others had done it, even someone *I* had helped over a few stiff hurdles. Aileen, who was my confidante when I lived in the Manse in Berwickshire, had been working on her book intermittently for years, with many falterings and back-slidings. Now that it was safely published, I felt it was partly *my* book, and that Aileen, if she had lived, would have encouraged me to 'get on with it', as I had always told her.

Aileen and I had always kept closely in touch, and thankfully she lived to see her book published. Even came to Glasgow to visit me one weekend. I put her up in the old Waverley Hotel where I had spent my first night, and we giggled our way through the soggy meals and talked our heads off.

Aileen wanted to see the city so I took her to the Necropolis, of all places: an immense cemetery near the Cathedral where all the mighty had been buried and were hemmed down by enormous sarcophagi toppling sideways with age. Some were so outlandish, we found it difficult to control our mirth, even on such holy ground. We came across some familiar names – offshoots of the Collins family, and a William Collins who had been a teetotal Lord Provost and whose nickname was 'Water Willie'.

So – I had encouraged Aileen and now that she was gone, I would have to encourage myself. 'If only I could find the time.' I stopped saying this when I discovered that almost everyone I met was convinced *they* could write a book 'if only . . .' Time, not talent, it appeared was all that was required to write a best seller.

In due course I was invited to join a more august body than the Writers' Club, called the PEN club (poets, editors, essayists, novelists) where I could look with awe on the really 'big' writers in Scotland. I was thrilled to sit at Sir Compton Mackenzie's feet listening to his fascinating tales. It was like being back in the byre with Jessie saying: 'Sit still an' I'll tell ye a story aboot a bubblyjock.' Only Monty's were true tales, about his sister Fay Compton, meeting D. H. Lawrence, buying an island, visiting Somerset Maugham, writing *The Four Winds of Love*. And never once had he to tell me to sit still.

I met an irascible poet called C. M. Grieve (Hugh MacDiarmid) and a gentle one called Edwin Muir. And I was soon on speaking terms with William Power, Eric Linklater, Neil Gunn and George Blake (whom I called Uncle George).

I also met many visiting speakers whose names I knew only from the title pages of their books, Hugh Walpole among them. Gradually I became accustomed to writers as 'ordinary' human beings, some very human. I remember sitting at a top table with J. B. Priestley when he leaned across to me and whispered: 'See all those folk glowering at us!' (They were looking at *him* not at *me*.) 'D'you think any of them ever *read*?'

I was not bold enough to say to him: 'They're reading something right now, Mr Priestley. Your face!'

*It* was a storybook in itself.

94

# 11. Scattered Showers

The writing I liked best to read was Jessie's. At long intervals she penned a postcard to me or one of her stilted letters.

'I am fine. How are you? I hope you are eating well and wearing your warm vest. Phemie is not improving. She is a stupid article. Yours faithfully, Jessie.' Sometimes she added a P.S.: 'Hope to see you soon.'

Since Jessie had never been one to show her feelings, it was the postscript that touched my heart. So I went home as often as I could at weekends and was relieved when she scolded the servant-girl – and me – as nippily as ever. But I noticed a strained look on her face and she could not conceal her limp as she trailed about on the stone kitchen floor. I had to use all my guile to get her to sit down for a few moments.

'Tell me, Jessie . . .' I tried to persuade her to look back to the time when I was a bairn. Anything to get her to sit still.

'A *bad* bairn,' she grumped; but when she started reminiscing some of the strain left her face and her eyes looked brighter as she recalled episodes I had long forgotten.

'Aye! Ye were a *bad* bairn,' she always ended.

'Well, see what a good job you've made of me!' said I, jumping down from the table.

'There's plenty room for improvement!' Jessie bit her lip as she rose to her feet. 'Ye're a perfect pest keepin' me from ma work. Get oot ma road!'

With Jessie cutting me down to size, there was no fear of my becoming bigheaded. So I did not boast about having started to write that book. (Yes! I *had* made a start: well begun was half done!) So I told her instead of my various attempts to find a suitable lodging in Glasgow, for at long last I was moving my tent.

It had been no wrench to leave that dingy back room at the Colmans', to escape from those terrible teas, from Wee Letty's sticky fingers and Mr Colman's unwelcome attentions. I just picked a place at random from the evening paper and went, not waiting to wonder if I might be throwing myself out of the frying pan into the fire.

Certainly I acquired a more flowery address: c/o Lovely, Woodfield Road; but all in the garden was far from lovely. Before long I discovered that not only did my landlady not live up to her name, she was not even *Mrs* Lovely.

Where the real one was I never found out; but I did wonder why the woman was always so angry. She raged at the two children (hers? his? whose?), she hissed like a viper at Mr Lovely, and dumped down the dishes in front of me as if she hated the sight of me.

After a week it became mutual till I began to think the Colman household was a peace-haven in comparison; and I dreaded the thought of returning to that madhouse every night. Then one evening as I put my key in the lock I heard the sound of laughter from inside. The children were playing in the hallway and shrieking with pleasure.

'She's away!' the boy said to me, as if that explained everything.

'Who?'

'The woman!' said the girl who was about to turn a somersault. She did not quite make it so I had a good view of her grubby drawers before Mr Lovely came out of the kitchen with an apron round his middle. He, too, looked happier, but refrained from standing on his head. All he said was, 'I'm making other arrangements.'

'So am I,' I thought to myself.

I was beginning to feel like a nomad as I hurriedly repacked my belongings and went searching for a new abode. This time I came to rest in a tenement flat in West Princes Street up a million stairs – I was always too puffed to count them – in a back room looking down-down-down on nondescript rooftops. On a good day, if I risked my neck by hanging out of the window upside down, as it were, I could catch a glimpse of some far-off hills; but it was too tricky an operation to indulge in every day.

Unbeknownst to myself, I had landed in a tenement which had once been the scene of a notorious crime. It was Duncan, my office friend, who enlightened me when he heard of my new address.

'That's where old Miss Gilchrist lived before she was murdered.'

'Mercy me!' said I, startled. 'Who murdered her?'

'Oscar Slater, so it was said, though it was never proved. He went to jail and then was reprieved,' Duncan told me. 'You're awful ignorant.'

He was right about that. The only other Oscar I had heard of was Oscar Wilde, and he went to jail, too, so for a time I confused the two.

Though I gained a bit of notoriety myself by living in such a den of iniquity, there was nothing murderous about my new landlady except that, like Mrs Colman, she did her best to poison me by her sloppy cooking. And in the end I became so disgusted with unwholesome meals, that I decided to take the biggest step of all. I would rent a furnished flat and 'do for myself'. It would be wonderful to bake scones and cook a tasty kipper if I fancied it.

But the most important thing of all was to get on with the book I had just started to write.

It was already beginning to take shape since the hero 'stotted into my head' one day when I was riding on one of Glasgow's shoogly tram-cars. It was pouring with rain, and though *I* was dry enough I could see plenty of foot-sloggers who were soaked to the skin. Particularly a ragged message-boy who was kicking a stone along the pavement. His loaded message-basket seemed too heavy for his thin arms to carry. Yet he lugged it along cheerfully enough, pausing now and again to give the stone another kick. Obviously a grocer's boy on his way to deliver a load of 'messages' to a customer.

'Poor wee soul!' I thought pityingly. Then I saw his face and knew he wasn't kicking a stone along a wet pavement. He was kicking the winning goal for Scotland! As he gave it a final swipe and it sailed high into the air I could almost hear the cheers.

'Hooray! Hooray! Well done, Macpherson!'

I have no idea why I called him Macpherson. It just came. The name seemed to suit him and though I never clapped eyes on that particular message-boy again, he has lived with me for many a long year, and even today his adventures are still in print, even in a Russian translation.

My original objective was to write a story that might show children they need not be rich – except in imagination – to live a full and adventurous life. I gave Macpherson a smattering of Jessie's rummlegumption and a little bit of *my* daft character – and after that, of course, *he* took over and went his own way.

In any case, he became the hero of that first book which ebbed and flowed in between the traumas of my daily stint at the office. And in between the birth of another character destined to hang round my neck like an albatross. Only *he* was a fish not a bird. His name was – and still is – Tammy Troot.

*Tommy Trout* would have been his name, I suppose, had he been an English fish. (A trout in Scotland is a *troot* and *Tammy* the Scottish equivalent of Tommy. Therefore, for better or worse, he is *Tammy Troot*.)

But little did I dream when I penned my first fishy story for BBC's Children's Hour that Tammy Troot would take over my life to such an extent and become so real that for years I was put off eating fish. I used to slink past the fishmonger's averting my eyes in case I met the reproachful gaze of Katy Kipper, Mrs Haddock or Sam Sole. Or heard them wailing, 'Help! Don't eat *us!*'

So I didn't for many a year; but now I can eat a kipper, or even a trout, without turning a hair! And though Tammy Troot has established himself it almost seems he has done it on his own, without my help.

Though all this was of vital interest to me, something much more important was happening in the wider world.

War had broken out. And my whole life was turned tapsulteerie (upside down).

Bombs would soon fall on Glasgow; and Mifs L. Derwent received urgent scrawls from Jessie and her parents. 'Come home! It's not safe in Glasgow.'

Nonsense! Fired with patriotic fervour, my main objective was to join up. But all the able-bodied men at the office had disappeared to do the same. So it was dinned into me where my duty lay. I must stay at my post – and work several times harder – taking over some of the absentees' tasks in order to keep the wheels running smoothly. And if I had a desperate desire to help my country, I could do something in my spare time, like serve in the canteen of an officers' club.

So I looked out Jessie's apron but did not join an officers' club. Instead, I found one called the Lion Club which catered for 'ordinary' soldiers and seamen. *They* were braver than lions, I thought, especially those who arrived wrapped in blankets after being torpedoed. They came in all shapes and sizes, grateful to be given cups of tea, slices of bread and marge, and occasional pies, chips and sausages.

Some, alas! were absent without leave; and when the Military Police came to pick them up, I had to restrain myself from hiding them in the boiler-house.

For the first part of my 'shift' I washed dishes in an underground, beetle-infested kitchen. I was glad it was hard work, for it made me feel I was winning the war as I rubbed and scrubbed up to the elbows in soapy water. No sooner was a batch of dishes washed, dried and packed on to an old-fashioned hoist than a shout came from above. 'HOIST!' We had to propel it aloft by painfully pulling at a heavy rope. Then we heard the clean dishes being taken off and another clatter as the dirty dishes came down. It was Up-down, Up-down with never a breathing space in between. Sometimes I wondered if it would be easier to 'join the war' and drive a tank.

The rest of my shift were nice friendly females, except for one: the supervisor, the one paid member of the team. Discipline was her strong point, and whether we were 'ladies' or not, she was not going to stand any nonsense. Not that we had time for capers. But I remember being ticked off for making a joke. 'Miss Derwent! Stop laughing!' Looking back on it now, it *all* sounds like a joke. Not then.

After doing a stint in the kitchen we had to go aloft to serve the men in the canteen. This involved wiping the sweat off our brows, tidying our tresses and putting on clean pinnies. It was difficult bridging the gap between being friendly with the man and not *too* friendly in case they 'took liberties'. Many of them, being so far from home, were looking for sympathetic companionship, if nothing else; so I lent an ear when I could and sometimes helped them to write letters home to their families. But I could not accept their constant invitations to the pictures or to the 'Barras'. I think they considered *me* somewhat retarded, for when one of them invited me out for a bevvy I had to ask, 'What's that?' It was a more worldly member of our shift who told me: 'It's a drink, softy! He wants to take you to a pub.'

Sometimes the 'boys' would bring us bars of chocolate which we shared around and devoured gratefully; but there were no rich gifts for us like those we heard about in the officers' canteens. An onion or a banana would have been as great a treat to us as silk stockings were to them.

I was often so exhausted that when going

home by tramcar I fell fast asleep and woke in the pitch dark of the blackout to find I was the only one on board.

Sometimes it was the All Clear that woke me and I realized there must have been an air-raid warning and the wardens had missed me when ushering the others into underground shelters. By that time I didn't much care if I was hit by a bomb. It would be a rest.

At home my old attaché case, still tied up with string, stood by my bedside every night, filled with manuscripts and a few indispensables, ready to act as a fleeing-case if a hasty evacuation became necessary. Our ears were constantly attuned to that terrible sound of the *sigh-reen*, as the Glasgow people called the siren.

I remember being asked in after-years by someone who had been in the Forces, 'What did *you* do during the war?'

The only reply I could think of was, 'Nothing.' But I still have the smallest badge in the world, marked LION CLUB to prove I did *something*.

# 12. Foreign Fields

At intervals someone with a welcome voice would ring me from the BBC: Auntie Kathleen demanding another story about Tammy Troot for Children's Hour. War or no war, young people – and Grannies too – still wanted stories to entertain them.

'But be careful not to mention this and that,' I was warned. Every comma had to be censored, and I could no longer walk through the portals of Broadcasting House without being escorted by an armed guard who never let me out of his sight.

'What d'you think I might do?' I once asked him. 'Broadcast to the nation? STOP THE WAR BY ORDER OF TAMMY TROOT!' But there was not a flicker of a smile on his face. Orders were orders, and he was forced to treat me as if I was one of Hitler's most dangerous spies.

So I wrote 'careful' stories but tried to make them as comical as I could, feeling that Tammy Troot was doing his little bit to win the war.

I had to turn a deaf ear to the call of the countryside, except at long intervals when I made the journey back home for a stolen weekend. There was a great deal of stopping and starting, of lying flat on the floor of the train during air-raid warnings, of guessing which station we were approaching in the blackout, and the terror of descending into a hedge or ditch in unknown territory. But all horrors were forgotten, of course, when eventually the familiar homestead hove in sight and I could smell the savoury food cooking by the kitchen fire.

I felt like the Prodigal Daughter when I learned that the herd had killed a sheep in my honour. I should have felt sorry for the poor beast but the roast was so tasty that my guilt quickly vanished. Alas! so did my appetite after a few mouthfuls. 'I ken what's wrang wi' *you*, lassie,' declared Jessie. 'Your stamoch's shrunk.'

True enough, if I had been thin before, I was a skinnymalink by now; but never mind that: it was music to hear Jessie scolding me. For how much longer, I wondered? The dreaded word *retire* was mooted more and more, and Jock-the-herd was on the look out for a cottage in the district where the family could end their days together in peace.

Who was I to begrudge Jessie her final years

of freedom? It was not so much for *my* sake as for *hers* that I railed against the inevitable, knowing how little she liked to sit at ease doing nothing. But her tongue would always be active and she gave me the benefit of it on my few wartime visits home.

Sometimes I was too tired to sleep at nights, and I remember lying flat out on the hillside one day in a kind of stupor, neither awake nor asleep. I half-heard Jock calling to the collies: 'In ahint! Leave the lassie alane. She's oot for the coont!' As if I was a boxer having been dealt a knock-out blow!

Such visits were few and far between, for once on the treadmill it was easier to keep going than to break off and have to start up the engine again.

But, of course, I survived. All bad things come to an end.

When the war was over I took a deep breath and tried to pick up the threads. What had I been doing *before*? Oh! writing that book! Well, get on with it, I told myself, much as I used to encourage Aileen when *she* was faltering. But *she* had had whole empty days in which to write and I could only steal odd moments, for by now I was so caught up in that Collins treadmill that I had almost forgotten my own identity.

Though I was being treated less as an employee, more like 'one of them', I was careful not to overstep the mark. Remember your place, I warned myself, though never sure what my place was.

The accolade was to be bidden to lunch in the board-room, an honour that fell to my lot at infrequent intervals. Fancy drinking dry sherry with the biggest bosses! There was always an uneasy feeling at the back of my mind. Why had I been invited? Could this be a gentle way of giving me the sack? If so, would I be glad or sorry? I could never make up my mind about my love-hate feeling for the firm.

Usually I did not get beyond the soup before all was revealed: often a subtle suggestion that I wouldn't mind doing a rush job. Who else could do it as well and as quickly? Of course, I would be given every facility, and even if I had to work late some nights (every night!) I could make up for it later on. They never told me how. Of course, I did it. Well! wasn't it an *emergency*?

There were times when I was bidden because someone I knew, lunching with the mighty, had specially asked to meet me. I remember Uncle Mac – Derek McCulloch from the BBC – falling on my neck, to the surprise of Good old Billy, who was astonished when we chit-chatted ten to the dozen about Children's Hour characters, including Toytown favourites and even Tammy Troot. I think they – Billy and Co. – were quite unaware that their minions led lives of their own outwith the firm.

The Chairman's mother, the Dowager, was full of life and vitality at the age of eighty. So much so, it was a relief when she went sailing round the world, as she did off and on every year, and kept the Captain and crew in order instead of her long-suffering family. She longed to have more says (some say, *any* say!) in the running of the firm and would have taken over the helm at the drop of a hat.

*She* could have done everything much better. 'I'd sack half of them on the spot,' she used to say to me behind her hand. She was a great one for making bullets and asking someone else to fire them. But: 'No, no, NO!' I had to say, petrified. 'NO! I couldn't!'

She remained more or less friendly with me. I was someone to talk to when the others wouldn't listen; and I think Good old Billy was quite pleased to be relieved of the burden now and again.

So I had my uses in the firm.

One day when I had been bidden to dine in the board-room they got as far as the pudding before revealing the reason for inviting me. I was puzzled, for there were no strangers present, just the family, and I had not been asked to undertake any impossible task in the next few days.

I was beginning to relax and Mrs Marzipan, the cook, was dishing out the apple dumpling when the blow fell. The cook was not really called Mrs Marzipan or Mrs Anybody. Her real name was Aggie Cleg; but when she put on her white apron and stuck out her pouter chest, I always thought of her as Mrs Marzipan. Though, no doubt, a more appropriate name would have been Mrs Roly-Poly.

The Directors had a penchant for sticky puddings – a prep-school hangover? – and Mrs Marzipan obliged by providing syrup sponges, treacle tarts, roly-polys and spotted dicks. Though I enjoyed the puddings I always found myself nid-nodding at my desk after a helping of Aggie Cleg's special.

Today I had just dug my spoon into the apple dumpling when the Chairman said in a casual voice: 'So how would you like to go to Egypt?'

'Egypt!' I gasped.

'Cairo,' said Good old Billy, shaking sugar on his dumpling.

'*Cairo!*' I could only repeat it like a zombie.

The Chairman began to explain, but he might as well have been quoting an upside-down telephone directory for all the sense I made of it. It was a long while before I could take in the facts; that a representative of the firm had been invited to attend a conference in Cairo, and that the purpose of the gathering was to discuss the provision of suitable books in English for young Egyptians to read.

Collins already did some trade with Egypt but were anxious to expand the market. That was why it was important that their rep. (me!) should listen carefully to the discussions and make suggestions, then agree to collaborate in the writing of a book with an Egyptian co-author.

Help! No wonder Mrs Marzipan's apple dumpling stuck in my gullet.

'You deserve a change,' said Good old Billy, swallowing the last drop of his coffee at the end of the meal. 'We'll fix you up in a nice hotel and, of course, Uncle Walter'll be on hand to keep an eye on you. It'll be a nice break.'

So that's what it was to be. A nice break!

All sorts of foolish notions flashed through my head about Egypt, which I had heard of but only in a Biblical kind of way. How far away was it from Scotland, what colour were the natives, did they speak our language, and how on earth would I get there?

By air, I was told. In an aeroplane!

No! No! I had never been off the ground before and would be petrified to fly to such an unlikely place as *Egypt*. Certainly there would be no need to get a return ticket for I would never ever see Scotland again.

I had myself dead and buried on alien soil before I got back to the office to take up my mundane task of writing 'poetry' to fill in gaps in a storybook. The words that came to mind were Cairo and Uncle Walter. They did little to help me with verses about Porky the Pig.

Though I knew little about Egypt I had heard a great deal about Uncle Walter. Not that I believed all the stories. They were too far-fetched, more suited to a Collins Adventure Annual than to a flesh-and-blood member of the family.

The Chairman's uncle, it was said, was a kind of remittance man who could not settle to any ordinary job, a swashbuckling character who had been through umpteen extraordinary adventures – the details varied – and who was at present the uncrowned king of Cairo attached to Reuter's Agency.

Uncle Walter had had a variety of wives (or were they concubines?) the present one being a beautiful Syrian called Mimi. As for slaves, he had one dozen, two dozen, or just dozens, one of whom slept on the floor outside his bedroom door every night. With a dagger, of course, in his teeth!

I was not comforted to think that *this* flamboyant creature was to be my philosopher and friend, but consoled myself with the thought that the stories were exaggerated. (*Au contraire* in many instances, I was to discover. Yet, in the event, Uncle Walter and I got on a treat.)

Meantime, I had homelier matters to worry about, like packing and saying goodbye to my friends whom I was certain I would never see again in this vale of tears. I had three weeks in which to prepare myself for The End, during which time I had to get 'jabs' against all sorts of weird diseases which were sure to kill me if the air crash didn't.

And, having gone through my private Gethsemane, I emerged pretending to be jaunty. 'Oh yes! I'm off to Egypt,' I said casually. 'Isn't it fun?' (I almost convinced *myself*!).

The first thing I packed was my hot-water bottle. After all, it was winter in Scotland – indeed, I left in a snowstorm – but when the Sudanese servant who had been allocated to me unpacked in the sweltering heat of Cairo, his big brown eyes goggled at the sight of it. He held it up, turning it this way and that, and looked at me for enlightenment. We had no words in common so I could only shake my head, at which he shook the bottle and hung it carefully at the side of the mirror where it remained throughout my stay in Egypt.

Nobody had told me whether to take hot clothes or cold clothes, what the climate would be like, what pitfalls to avoid and how to cope with strange foreign money. The only communication I had was a hurried scrawl from Uncle Walter saying that he was off to the Middle East on business but hoped to be back in time to welcome me at Heliopolis when (if) I arrived in the one piece.

So I concentrated instead on the business side of my mission, determined to cut a sensible figure at the conference and to get my facts and figures as correct as possible. I wrote out reams of suggestions for books I might produce with a 'collaborator', prepared if necessary to write them in pidgin English since I had not a word of basic Egyptian. (What language *did* they speak?) I feared the natives would not understand my broad Scots tongue; and in this, if in nothing else, I was right.

Indeed, I was still speaking pidgin English when I came home. When someone asked me how I had liked being in Egypt, I replied: 'Was good. I enjoy.'

There was no time for a Border foray before I left, for as it happened I had committed myself to my 'big flit' from West Princes Street: my removal to a semi-furnished flat in Botanic Crescent which was to be a happy haven for many years to come.

It was a four-footed flitting. I removed with the help of a horse-drawn lorry lent by a friend who had inherited her father's business. Jean was a woman ahead of her time, who had taken on a man's responsibilities and made a great success of being a female boss in a male world. Her employees respected as well as feared her. *I* looked up to her for she was far above me in stature as well as in rummlegumption; but she had a soft centre and was forever helping waifs and strays like myself.

I had encountered Jean at the Soroptimist Club which I had been invited to join, a sorority where members of different 'categories' met and mingled in friendly fellowship. We had representatives from every branch of art and industry: a lady policeman, a lady conjuror, a lady minister. Everything except a lady hangwoman. We were all *ladies*. Not a full-blooded male in sight; so how we perked up and put on our best hats when we heard a Rotary Club speaker was coming to address us!

Jean, who was President of the Club, had no time for fancy hats. She treated men and women alike and preferred horses. For a long time after her father died she refused to mechanize the business. I once saw into her musty ledger-room where an ancient Bob Cratchit was scratching away with a pronged pen. Dickens would have been proud of him!

In spite of her old-fashioned methods Jean ran an efficient business, and later when she acquired a fleet of motor-lorries became a leading light in the city. But a horse-drawn van was sufficient to transport my few belongings from West Princes Street to a backwater in Botanic Crescent, where I felt I could settle down like a squirrel and build a cosy nest. It was another roof-top flat but with a leafy view of the nearby Botanic Gardens and *birdsong* to be heard in the early morning – the nearest thing to the countryside in the middle of the city.

Here was a haven where at last I could find peace to write my books.

But I needed *time* and I was still beset by duties, the first of which was to fly away to Egypt.

# 13. Flight Into Egypt

It seemed strange to be sitting up in the strato-
sphere peeling a Cox's Orange Pippin, one of
the few edible items I could find on the plastic
tray in front of me.

I was miles above the world, away, away
above the clouds, almost in heaven. The clouds,
white and fluffy, seemed to be enticing me to
leave the aeroplane and go for a stroll, stepping
from one to the other on my bare feet like an
angel. It was all so unreal, I was not sure whether
I was alive or dead. It didn't really matter any
more.

At last I was on my way to Egypt, the weeks
of preparation over.

For better or worse I had packed a variety of
garments, including woolly vests and jumpers
(along with my hot-water bottle) so I was

prepared, I thought, for all eventualities. In my purse I had some strange foreign money, doled out to me by Mr Robb from the Counting House, who cautioned me over and over again to be careful with it, as if I would suddenly blow the lot on buying a pyramid or a couple of camels. I had letters of credit, letters of introduction to strange Egyptian dignitaries, letters for Uncle Walter, and a hand-written one from Good old Billy. 'Be sure to take plenty of time off and enjoy yourself.'

Fancy that!

But, of course, I would never get there. All very well for him sitting in the board room eating one of Mrs Marzipan's roly-polies. High up in the firmament it was the 'plane that was doing the roly-poly before plummeting down to the ground, leaving my stomach behind. Ta-ta, Cox's Orange Pippin! Goodbye, world . . .

A disembodied voice was talking to us. God from heaven? Or the Devil from the other place?

'There is no need for alarm. We have had to overshoot the runway. It was not possible to land at Heliopolis owing to a white mist engulfing the airport. But don't worry; we'll soon find another landing-place. Better keep your seat belts fastened. We apologize . . .'

No cause for alarm! Of course not! A nun across the passage from me was telling her beads. But what was she telling them? I counted my fingers, surprised to find they still added up to ten. Think of something *real*, I told myself.

What about Auld Baldy-Heid at the village school in the Borders? *He* was the one who first taught me to count up to ten, though sometimes I copied the shepherd's rigmarole way of adding up the sheep.

> Een-teen-tethera-methera-pimp.
> Awfus-dawfus, deefus, dumfus-dik . . .

I clenched my fists as if to fend off the sting of the teacher's strap, but in reality to hold myself together as the 'plane juddered to the ground.

'It's all right,' said God – or the Devil. 'We have landed at Fayed in the Canal Zone. This airport is controlled by the Egyptians. Obey their instructions.'

Certainly! Especially as they came on board fingering their guns. When they demanded our passports we gave them up without a murmur. 'Out!' We all trooped out into the desert, and for the first time in my life I experienced a really *hot* sun. It was early morning and the great red monster was rising in the sky like a fiery furnace ready to shrivel us all up.

Fayed was a small airstrip used by the Allies during the Battle of El Alamein (I remembered hearing *that* name mentioned on the wireless during the war). Since the coup which overthrew Neguib, now under house arrest, the Egyptians had kicked all except a nucleus of Britons out of the country; and it was some of those left-over British troops who rescued us from that fiery furnace, took us into one of their large huts and conjured up a 'breakfast' of sorts.

Mine consisted of a saucerful of pineapple chunks which did little to assuage my thirst.

117

Meantime there were uneasy whispers amongst the passengers. What were the Egyptians up to? When would they let us go? Would they give us back our passports? We tried to ask the Cockney lad who was doling out the pineapple chunks. He informed us that one never knew with the Egyptians. Best to humour them. They could keep us here for days if it came up their humps, or we might be off as soon as they had refuelled. *If* there was any fuel . . .

Luckily, I told myself, this was only a dream. It was not really happening! Yet, why was I beginning to melt? Drip, drip, drip! The perspiration rolled down my brow like a small rivulet. There was no air-conditioning in the hut, no shelter outside from that scorching sun, nothing growing in the sandy desert but a giant cactus. The tiny one I nurtured in a pot at home was like Tom Thumb in comparison. From then on I took against cactuses for life and got rid of my 'baby' as soon as I got home.

The captain of the 'plane was keeping a stiff upper lip, and we all followed his example, though everyone's schedules were up the spout and there was no opportunity of telephoning to explain our absence. The Cairo papers were already printing an ominous headline: 'PLANE MISSING IN THE DESERT'

Poor Mr Robb! All that funny money gone and nothing to show for it. But I had no time to be sorry for *him*. I was melting so rapidly I would soon be only a puddle on the floor. The Egyptian came and went at intervals and appeared to be counting us. 'Een-teen-tethera-methera . . .', seldom getting the same answer twice especially if we had changed places. The kind Cockney chap offered me some tinned peaches but I shook my head, scattering another shower of drip-drops from my brow. The nun was either dead or asleep, hidden under her habit, and the rest of the passengers stared into space thinking their own thoughts.

Four hours? Or five? Then suddenly the captain, followed by his navigator, strolled into the hut whistling under his breath. 'I think it's OK for you to go on board. Take your places quietly. I'll try to get hold of your passports, and will distribute them later. Good luck!'

When I got up I found I had lost the use of my legs. I supported the nun, or she supported me and we trailed across the burning sand to the 'plane which was shivering and shaking, showing signs of being alive and ready for take-off.

It was wonderful when we went on board to be sitting in softer seats and presently to feel the air-conditioning seeping through. And we could breathe even more freely when the captain brought round an armful of passports. He gave me the nun's by mistake but we quickly did a swap else *she* might have been excommunicated for changing her appearance, though *I* would have been quite pleased to go home looking purer than the driven snow.

We flew low over the desert on our way back to Cairo. I blinked my eyes in disbelief when I looked down and saw a storybook scene: a camel cavalcade wending its way towards a watering-hole. I almost clapped my hands with pleasure at the sight of it; though I still could not believe it was all real.

Yes! It must be! The Nile was snaking its way across the sand, and there were the Pyramids looming up . . . 'Fasten your seat-belts!' We had arrived at Heliopolis.

A million folk were milling around the airport but none looking for me. I longed for the sight of a familiar face – even Mr Robb from the Counting House would have done – but there was not a single soul in the whole of Egypt who would know me. Hold on! A garbled voice was speaking over the intercom. 'Miss Derwent! Message for Miss Derwent!'

That was *me*.

I was to go to the Enquiry Desk; and there awaiting me were two dark-skinned gents wearing red fezzes and black tail-coats who bowed low at my approach and presented an attractive looking veiled lady. Mimi, Uncle Walter's third, fourth, or fifth wife? A Syrian who spoke enough pidgin English to put me in the picture.

Uncle Walter, I discovered, had not been able to wait for the delayed 'plane but she (Mimi) was here to welcome me with two friends: Dr Somebody and the Minister of Something. More bows from the red fezzes – and that was us introduced.

Meantime, minions were attending to my luggage and tickets; then I was swept out of the airport and into a long, long car.

I sat in a daze between Dr Somebody and

Mimi and watched the unlikely landscape sweep by. 'A banyan tree.' Mimi spoke at intervals to explain this and that. 'A mosque. Look! That's where the Mouski is. Big market . . .' Presently: 'We're here! This is your hotel. Don't worry! The servants will take care of everything. We'll call for you tonight at nine o'clock to take you to the cinema. . . .'

The cinema! Fancy coming all this way just to go to the pictures!

There were two servants assigned to look after me at the hotel, as black as ebony, and as tall as giants in their long white gowns. One was called Aziz, the other Hassan, and they were father and son, but they both seemed the same age so I could never figure out which was which. I just nodded and grinned at them, and they nodded and grinned back while extracting the crumpled contents of my luggage. I was too tired to be ashamed of my messy packing, and eventually lay down in the darkened bedroom, but when I closed my eyes the bed began to waltz round a giant cactus, so that I had to cling on for dear life to prevent myself from being tossed out . . .

A lifetime later one of the servants (*père* or *fils*) rattled me awake by tapping a spoon on a tray at my bedside. Food and drink were to be dispensed, and I must pull myself awake to get ready for Mimi who, I vaguely remembered, was to take me to the cinema.

She arrived with her two companions in the same long, long car but dressed in more elegant garments and drenched in fragrant perfume. I had put on a 'good' frock but had no idea what

I looked like. I was suffering, I suppose, from jet-lag and my most pressing problem was how to keep awake. The next thing I knew we were in a box in a theatre and the fezzed gentlemen were bowing to their acquaintances on all sides. Mimi had discarded her veil and was smoking a tiny black cigarette, and I was offered sticky sweetmeats from a silver dish.

The film was in English with Arabic sub-titles, a simple enough love story – *Three Coins in a Fountain* – but I could not follow it. There were too many other interesting sights to be seen in the audience.

'You are not enjoying?' my companions accused me.

'Oh yes, I *am* enjoying,' I protested, and tried to turn my attention to the screen.

Don't fall asleep, I warned myself! The fezzed gents were wide awake and enjoying *them*selves. Who was I to spoil their fun? The evening was just beginning for them. They would take me to supper later, they told me. I was far too thin; they must fatten me up. (*Everybody* in Egypt wanted to fatten me up as if to get me ready for market.) Then they would take me to see the belly-belly dancers. I would enjoy.

When I had seen one tummy gyrating in all directions I had seen the lot. The repetitive movements and the tom-tom beat of the music had a hypnotic effect on me. I was sound asleep with my eyes open making feeble responses to my escorts' polite conversation. 'Oh no!' shaking my head. 'Not tired!'

I drank a small cup of bitter black coffee and

chewed the grounds while watching someone smoking a hubble-bubble pipe. It was all so different from the farmhouse kitchen at home, I was sure I must be dead, and longed to be left to Rest In Peace.

I have no recollection of the end of the evening, but it must have ended for in due course I woke up in my hotel bedroom and discovered when I leapt out of bed that I was half undressed. And the reason I leapt out and ran to the window in my bare feet was that I had been wakened by a strange noise in the street. I had heard nothing like it in my life before – like a hundred cross-cut saws searing through wood. What on earth could it be? I rushed to the window to find out. The fact that there was a dark gentleman in my room picking up my slippers did not deter me.

'What is it? What's that noise?' I demanded, half-thinking the world had come to an end.

Aziz – or Hassan – shook his head at me. Then he nodded it and pointed out of the window to a string of donkeys passing along the street. Donkeys! Could such innocent-looking creatures make a din like that? Yes, they could! As time went by I grew so accustomed to their alarum call every morning that the noise passed over my head and I never even noticed it. As for conversing with my two slaves, I gave up trying to make them understand by speaking LOUD, and relied on gestures instead. So in the end we were all speaking volumes with our hands.

On that first day I began to get to grips with Cairo. Uncle Walter was still missing but sent a message saying he would take me to the seminar which was to start the following day. Meantime, I was to be shown the local sights by a male-and-female couple of aides whose only attempt at speaking English was to say: 'Jo-lly good!' But, like Aziz and Hassan, they were jolly good gesticulators, so I followed them obediently, nodding and smiling when *they* nodded and smiled.

They took me first to the Menai House Hotel at the Pyramids to drink a *tasse* of the ever-popular (not with me) bitter black coffee. After which they hoisted me on to a camel.

'Wh-oo-oa!' I gasped as the beast gathered himself together and reared up to such a height he was almost as big as a pyramid itself.

The dragoman appeared to be a bit of a card in many languages, though not in mine. He evidently decided I was American and, hitting the camel on the rump, remarked: 'Very nice camel. Him called Pepsi-Cola.'

'Wrong c-c-country!' I spluttered, hanging on for dear life. 'I come from S-S-Scotland!'

'Him called Wheesky-Soda!' grinned the dragoman, quick as a flash, and gave the beast another whisk on the rump.

Wheesky-Soda and I remained attached to each other in spite of some near misses on the way down to view the Sphinx from closer quarters. Why was his nose bashed, I wondered? Or should it be *her*? The aides who were calmly riding their camels behind me explained every-thing by saying, 'Jo-lly good!' So that was my history lesson over.

In any case, I had to concentrate on Wheesky-

Soda who had a habit of collapsing in the sand
without giving me any warning. Doubtless he
had been trained to do so at certain special points
of interest, so that his customers could descend
and view the Great Pyramid, for example. I came
off several times willy-nilly and had to climb up
steep stone steps whether I wanted to or not, and
peer into dark dungeons. Meantime, outside, the
merciless sun beat down on me as if trying to
fry me sunny-side up.

'Jo-lly good!' my escorts said at intervals, and
as they paid off the dragoman he presented me
with a lucky scarab which I possess to this day.
It has brought me good luck and bad, like any
other 'magic' stone; but, if nothing else, it still
has the effect of central heating on me; for I have
only to look at it to feel again the bristling of
that baking sun.

On the way back to Cairo the aides suggested
several treats for my entertainment, one being a
visit to the belly-belly dancers. 'NO! I've been!'
I said so loudly that they could not fail to understand. What I wanted, I told them firmly, was a
simple meal in my hotel and an early night.

'Jo-lly good!'

They would accompany me and keep guard
while I consumed my meal, then we could dance
in the Starlight Room at the hotel. 'Music very
nice. Jo-lly good.'

I ate something or other while they looked on
and at intervals clapped their hands to summon
a minion to remove the plates. (I never became
accustomed to this autocratic method of dealing
with underlings, and over-did my 'pleases' and

'thank yous' in an effort to compensate.) The meal ended with the usual bitter black coffee.

'Could I not have some *tea*?' I pleaded.

'Jo-lly good!' said my escorts, but the tea never came.

They were eager to introduce me to the delights of the Starlight Room which was only a poky little place with a slippery floor. It had a glass ceiling with twinkling stars which went round and round all the time – or maybe I was the one who went round and round.

My male escort urged me to dance with him while his female companion looked on with approval, clapping her tiny hands and rolling her kohl-tinged eyes in time to the music. 'Jo-lly good!' It was a strange kind of dance, one step forward, another backward, twirl around and that was it! I began to feel like a belly-belly dancer myself. In another moment I would break into a Highland Fling and the twinkling ceiling would collapse on top of me.

'JO-LLY GOOD!' I said loudly to my companions and declared I was going to bed. 'Thank you! Good night!'

Hassan – or Aziz – was at my bedroom door, ready to usher me in and go through all that picking-up-the-slippers nonsense. 'NO!' I said, shutting the door on his face. 'I go sleep. Good night!'

The longest day, as Jessie used to say, inevitably comes to an end.

# 14. King of Cairo

Next day I discovered Uncle Walter truly *was* king of Cairo.

Fezzed heads bowed low at his approach and even the donkeys made way for his long car when it came hooting down the street. But His Nibs took no notice of man or beast and, if he was driving the car himself, put his foot on the accelerator and his hand on the hooter, so that I became accustomed to seeing bare heels springing out of his path just in the nick of time. 'Missed them!' I used to gasp, covering my eyes with my hands.

Uncle Walter was slow if he had to bother about doing some tedious task himself, but quick when he wanted others to bestir themselves. His tolerance level was too low to suffer fools gladly, and everything must be done immediately '*Now!*'

he would shout and everyone would jump to attention. He could not be bothered with the tricky little jobs in life, such as peeling off the outer covering from a packet of cigarettes. What were his aides for? He would fling the packet to one of them. 'Can't get it off. Open it for me. Now!'

In spite of his failings, I thought Uncle Walter was the Perfect Gentleman though, of course, he belonged to the pages of a story book rather than to real life. But as I was living an unreal life myself, I decided I might as well enjoy this Egyptian dream before waking up in gloomy Glasgow.

On that first day Uncle Walter and I sat in the back of his long car while a chauffeur drove us to the Ministry of Something (Education, it turned out to be) where the seminar was to be held.

It looked like a vast temple with marble floors, one room leading into another, and with throngs of white-robed people awaiting the Minister's pleasure. Had we taken our rightful places we would have been far down the queue, but Uncle Walter brushed past the lot, with me trotting behind him till he reached the Presence.

The Minister dismissed a roomful of suppliants to turn his attention to *us*. His conversation consisted mainly of 'Yes, yes!' interspersed with bows and smiles. Yes, yes! he agreed to everything Uncle Walter asked. Yes, yes! I was to be given pride of place at the seminar. It would be an honour to have a *lady* all the way from Scotland to grace their meetings. Yes, yes! he himself would conduct me round the book exhibition.

But first the seminar had to be opened with due ceremony by another Minister (of War, I think) after reviewing the troops assembling right now in the outside courtyard. Yes, yes! he would just have to change into his uniform and it would all be happening in half an hour *promptly*. (I soon learned there was no such word in the Egyptian language.)

I could hear the soldiers clattering about in the courtyard as we were conducted to the conference chamber. More fezzed heads bowed low as we entered and surprised eyes stared sideways at the pale-faced stranger with red hair. I was relieved to see there were already some females present – only three amongst that gaggle of men – each dressed in deep black and with downcast eyes. 'Who am I,' they seemed to be saying, 'compared with such noble creatures as *men*?'

Nonsense! I said to myself and held my head high. We're all *somebody*.

Before the half-hour had passed Uncle Walter grew tired of cracking his fingers, which had been his only occupation since we entered the chamber. 'I'm going out,' he whispered impatiently to me. 'You'll be all right!'

I had to be! Not knowing how to crack my fingers, I just concentrated on keeping awake; and at the end of another hour or so could hear promising sounds from outside. The soldiers were dropping their rifles, picking them up again and forming fours. But it was a false alarm. It could have been another hour – another *year*, it seemed – before I heard commands being shouted. At last the Minister had arrived and was reviewing the troops.

Presently he came marching in (promptly, three hours late), an insignificant wee man weighed down with medals, and received the obeisances of everybody except myself. I just looked down at my toes and hoped that would do.

He gabbled an opening speech in Arabic, then the Minister of Education attempted a few English phrases. He was 'constipated', he told us, and could not say much; but he welcomed us all, particularly the lady from Scotland. I felt I ought to get up, twirl round on my toes and blow a blast on the bagpipes.

I was presented to the War Minister who muttered something which might have been 'Stand at ease' for all I knew; then he went off surrounded by soldiers clutching their rifles. The other Minister (of Education) kept his promise to escort me round the book exhibition. To his surprise, I think, I took careful note of every-thing, and even pulled out a pad to jot down some reminders. After all, I was here to *work*, and felt I must do something to earn my keep.

We broke for refreshments: black coffee (what else!) and sweetmeats. Then the real seminar began, some of the speeches in French, which I tried to follow, and some in broken English. It was all merging into a strange *mélange* when suddenly it was all over for the day and we were set free. *Lowsed* Jessie would have said.

The black–gowned ladies broke rank and came

over to me, holding out tiny hands and twittering like three little maids from school. I was pleased to hear them speaking such passable English. One was called Bahia, whose age might have been anything between sixteen and sixty. The latter, I believe, since she was a senior lecturer and went round schools trying to teach teachers to teach! Another whom I called Oasis (because she became an oasis in the desert to me), I was surprised to hear speak fluent English; but then I discovered she had originally come from Yorkshire to marry an Egyptian: 'But he is gone.' Dead or just lost, I never found out.

The third member was the most silent of the group with no name I could recognize, yet felt *she* had an inner strength, and that there was more to her than to her garrulous companions.

Oasis, the ringleader, suggested they should all accompany me back to my hotel in Uncle Walter's car which was waiting in the courtyard. The chauffeur was sitting drowsing at the wheel and reluctantly pulled himself together at our approach. I think he felt we were carrying promptness a bit too far when he received several sets of instructions to drive back to the hotel *immediately*.

There, we all had TEA and as we sat and chatted over the cups a bond of friendship was established; and after that one or other of the trio kept an eye on me during my stay in Egypt. Bahia took me round some of her schools where I met hundreds of little Egyptian children, and clapped hands with them as we jogged around in the blazing sun. Oasis invited me home to her dark little flat which had a wonderful view of the Pyramids if one ever dared push the windows open, and told me her life story which might have come out of *Peg's Paper*. And the Silent One took me for a strange meal aboard a ship moored on the river Nile. I spoke less to her but I think I liked her best. It was pleasant to know they were *there* in the intervals of being ferried around by Uncle Walter or his minions.

I was allocated a permanent aide who walked unobtrusively behind me and who was just called You as far as I knew, and a companion who accompanied me when I went on sight-seeing expeditions. Uncle Walter referred to *him* as the General, and indeed he always wore a faded uniform with ribbons on his breast depicting old battles lost or won. There was some mystery about him, of course, but it was no use questioning it. I just accepted the General as he accepted me, and enjoyed his company. There was no doubt he had come out of a top drawer, like Uncle Walter, and it was evidently a Scottish top drawer, for though he had the usual educated Eton accent the lilt was still there. It became stronger when he was talking to me, asking to hear news of his home-land. On our expeditions it was the sole topic of conversation.

It was a pity, for I was eager to learn more about the local customs in Cairo, but the General wanted to hear what was happening on the river Clyde. I tried to dredge up information about the shipyards, about Scottish politics and about rugby. At the mention of the game, his eyes brightened and I felt he must have played for

Scotland in his day. I could almost see him in a torn jersey with bleeding nose. 'Go on, Jock! Kick him in the shins!' He also wanted to know about Balmoral where he had stayed with the Royal Family, and about the bonnie banks of Loch Lomond.

He could not sing but he would try to grunt the tune, and my Minder, walking behind me, would grunt, too, thinking it was a kind of game. Indeed, it was all a game, far removed from my normal life. I tried to bring some sanity to the situation by sending postcards home. If they ever got there, then this *was* reality and not a dream.

Jessie's card was the most difficult. By now she, with her brother Jock-the-herd, and her sister Joo-anne, was installed in their 'retired' cottage. I could visualize them sharing their one pair of spectacles as they read the card and peered at a picture of the Pyramids. 'This country reminds me of the Bible. I have ridden on a camel. I will soon be coming to see you.' I did not add, 'Wish you were here.' What on earth would Jessie do in this alien land with no homely kitchen fire to sit beside? I could not visualize her squatting all day under a banyan tree or riding a mule through the narrow alleyways of the Mouski.

I sent dispatches back to the firm in Glasgow and was heartened to receive a scratchy letter from Mr Robb to the effect that if I needed more money I had only to ask. Mercy goodness me! had he taken leave of his senses?

In fact, Uncle Walter was taking care of many

of my expenses, running up a fat bill, as I found out later when he sent it to Glasgow. It put me in a bit of a quandary, for how could I confess I had not even attended some of the gatherings arranged in my honour, or purchased some of the items included in his list? But Uncle Walter was not a rogue: he was only emulating some of his Egyptian colleagues who considered it the natural thing to make a 'bit on the side'. (But how could one explain *that* to Mr Robb?)

Mimi, too, did her best to entertain me. At least, she held a bridge party in my honour. It was attended by all the cronies with whom she normally played bridge plus a sprinkling of the fezzed fraternity. They clustered in little groups and gossiped about goodness knows what. How to make a bit on the side, perhaps.

I did not play bridge myself – a good enough reason for Mimi to hold a bridge party in my honour. But I was content to sit out with my shadow, the General, and gaze around at Uncle Walter's magnificent home. Well! It seemed magnificent to me, though doubtless it was the norm in well-to-do families in Cairo. Soft-footed servants in long robes handed round refreshments, and I was forced to sip the dreaded bitter coffee and nibble some over-sweet delicacies.

Sometimes the General, instead of asking me questions about Scotland, would go over and over a story (true, I think) of how he had been one of the first to enter Tutankhamen's tomb. He seemed to know a great deal about Tut, as he called him, had been on the dig, and could enumerate every item brought to light. Moreover, he promised to take me to the museum to see the treasures for myself. And he did. It was one of the most wonderful, though exhausting, days of my life.

I remember less about the treasures themselves than of the General's animated account of the discovery, and of how his voice became more Scottish as he grew more excited. It made me feel home-sick to hear him. Sometimes I longed for this strange episode to end, but I was caught up in a whirlpool of odd happenings.

In between my working visits to the Ministry, I was taken to functions in the Semirimas Hotel, at the Gezira Club, and to a fabulous outdoor luncheon on the banks of the river Nile where I was fanned by a kind of punka-wallah. No use worrying about expenses. Wait till the day of reckoning came.

I did try to make some sensible contribution at the Ministry and in my discussions with the educationists. Before I left I had agreed to write a book in conjunction with Bahia and, after visiting the largest bookshop in Cairo, fixed up a deal with the proprietor whereby Collins would send out consignments of suitable titles for the 'delectation', as he put it, of his customers.

How payment was to be made I hesitated to find out, but put him in touch with 'our Mr Robb' and hoped for the best.

I was not sure whether to be glad or sorry when my final week arrived and I had to think myself back into another world. I could not visualize Cathedral Street, Glasgow and had forgotten what Good old Billy looked like. (It was a trifle daunting on my return to hear him say: 'Oh, hullo! Back already?') as if he had never even noticed my absence!)

By now I was growing heartily sick of all those cloying sweetmeats and was growing thinner instead of plumper. Wait till I get home, I promised myself! I would have mince and tatties every day of the week and plenty of Mrs Marzipan's fattening puddings. It would be great to get back to the old familiar scenes. Yet, would I miss such sights in Cathedral Street as businessmen kneeling down to pray at the call of the muezzin, or colourful tribes trudging with their camels across the desert? Could I push all this to the back of my mind and get on with ordinary living in dull Scotland?

Yes, I could! I told myself, and began counting the days.

I began too, to think of presents to take home and went to the Mouski, suitably guarded, to make some purchases. I had no desire to haggle over such an insignificant item as a small brass donkey but the General insisted it was the done thing.

'They'll be disappointed if you don't,' he assured me; but I left it to him to do the transaction, since he spoke such fluent Arabic. And when the inevitable battle began, I stepped aside to keep out of the crossfire. It was obviously a ritual, that the General and the merchant should bawl at each other as the price soared or sank. They seemed to be growing angrier and angrier till I was sure they would take to fisticuffs; but suddenly it was all over and they ended up smiling almost in each other's arms. I was offered – oh yes! – a small glass of bitter coffee to seal the bargain, and after doling out my drachmas the donkey was mine.

What a palaver! I told the General I would sooner pay the full price, which appeared to be little enough, anyway, than go through all that rigmarole every time I made a purchase; but he said, 'Rubbish! It's only the bargaining that makes it bearable. Who would want to shop otherwise?'

All the same, it was not my idea of fun, so my shopping was much skimpier than I had hoped, and I contented myself with buying coloured necklaces, a brocade scarf, and a few 'lucky scarabs' for my friends. When I paid the full price the merchant was so surprised he almost fell down at my feet. Then he offered me – apart from coffee, of course – a little brass bell for nothing and a pair of Cleopatra earrings.

'So there!' I said defiantly to the General as we moved off; but he countered with, 'Cheap rubbish!' All the same, when I examined the Cleopatra earrings more closely I noticed they were stamped with a silver hallmark. So there, indeed! I have *them* to this day, too.

I wished I had brought more tartan souvenirs with me to pass on to the Egyptian friends who had been so kind to me. I took orders for the Trio (Bahia, Oasis, and the Silent One) for Scottish items I could send them when I got an opportunity. Bahia's were modest requests for a strange assortment of goods: a screwdriver, mustard, aspirin, and a pair of sharp scissors.

Oasis wanted a *real* woollen jersey, not so much to keep her cosy as to remind herself of colder weather at home, and the Silent One asked for a *klit*.

I translated this into *kilt*, but I knew she would never dare wear such a garment so decided to send her a tartan scarf instead. I was touched to receive so many going-away gifts myself and wondered how I would ever pack them into my suitcases. The General solved the problem by presenting me with a roomy hold-all which even though it was covered with garish scenes of Cairo, I accepted gratefully and used as a message-bag when I got back to Glasgow.

But of all the strange characters I met in Egypt it was Uncle Walter who took the biscuit. I could have watched him for ages as he blew hot or cold, for there was never any knowing what today's mood might be; though he was invariably courteous to me and took me in his long car on many unusual visitations.

I can never forget the Coptic wedding we attended together. The bridegroom was one of Uncle Walter's staff who had humbly begged his employer to come and be the 'chieftain' at the ceremony. Indeed, he was given much more prominence than the bridegroom himself. As for the bride she was the merest nonentity, a shrinking violet whose one desire was not to be noticed. The groom certainly paid no attention to her. He was waiting at the door to conduct us down the aisle with great ceremony and, after settling me in a seat of honour, he conducted

Uncle Walter on to the platform where he sat in
great state facing the audience.

I remember being presented with a little dish
of sugared almonds, listening to Uncle Walter
making a speech in Etonian English (which the
foreigners listened to in breathless silence though
they did not understand a word), and finally
being bowed back to the car by the now-married
bridegroom after declining to attend the jollifi-
cations which would follow.

Uncle Walter kept his temper throughout the
entire proceedings and even blessed the bride
with a chaste kiss on her forehead. Oh! well
done you! I thought, sucking a sugared almond.
You're a real trouper.

I saw Uncle Walter under many different lights
and could easily have become one of his devoted
slaves. He did make a half-hearted suggestion
about my staying on and taking control of his
office. My immediate reaction was to say a
euphoric 'Yes, yes!', but commonsense (Jessie's
rummlegumption) changed it into 'No, no!'

Mimi graciously gave a farewell bridge party
in my honour, and Uncle Walter presented me
with a specially made fez as a parting present. So
now I had what I had always wanted. A red hat!
But I never wore it except once at a fancy-dress
party.

I was embarrassed by all the tearful farewells.
Not being a weepy person myself, I was
surprised to see grown men and women spouting
waterfalls of tears at the mere mention of saying
goodbye.

'It's just their temperament,' the General told

139

me, blowing his own red nose. I must be as hard as nails, I told myself, for I remained dry-eyed to the end. Besides, I had been brought up not to show my feelings.

So, cheerio Cairo! It has been a wonderful experience but it's over. Back to Bonnie Scotland! Back to snow and hot-water bottles!

# 15. Back to Reality

Flying home, I was an old hand at air travel, so blasé that I told a trembling fellow-traveller sitting next to me: 'There's nothing to it. The best thing is to settle down and go to sleep.' I was a trifle miffed when she did just that, not awakening till the Argonaut Speedbird stopped for refuelling at Rome.

Meanwhile, I was left high and dry: *Sleep I could get nane.*

It was a night flight, leaving Heliopolis in the wee sma' hoors, and though I was not too apprehensive about the flight itself, I was too keyed-up after all the tearful farewells to 'fall over'. I could not even hunt in my hold-all for a book to read for by now my companion was not only sound asleep but had found a comfortable spot to rest her head on my shoulder. I sat still, not to disturb her, and presently in the semi–darkness met the quizzical gaze of the Captain as he strolled along the aisle.

'Not sleeping? Would you like a cup of tea?'

I gave a little nod, then I asked anxiously, 'Who's driving the 'plane?' We were talking in whispers, not to disturb the rest of the passengers which made the encounter seem more sinister; but the Captain was smiling. 'Oh! it's on automatic control. We call him George – so *he*'s doing the driving!'

'Go away!' I said in an urgent whisper. 'Hurry! And never mind about the tea.'

The idea of the 'plane flying all by itself through the night sky was too much for me to swallow; but I did swallow the tea which was brought later by a silent steward, and though it did not taste anything like *real* tea, it was better than bitter black coffee. And it helped to keep me even wider awake!

I slept the clock round in my London hotel, then woke and ordered a 'full English breakfast': bacon, egg, sausages, toast and marmalade. The smell was deliciously appetizing, but after the first few bites, I was sated. I would have to work myself gradually back into normal meals – but at least I had enjoyed the smell!

But oh! It was a COLD world. When I got back to Glasgow I could not get enough of hot-water bottles and winter woollies. And I became a bit of a bore extolling the delights of the Egyptian sun (I had already forgotten how blistering it could be), the strawberries, the exotic flowers, the colourful characters – till suddenly I got sick of the whole subject myself and tucked it away at the back of a drawer along with my ornamental fez.

At the first opportunity I visited the Borders. My parents were pleased enough to see me, but it was scarcely worth my while giving them the tawdry gift I had brought, for they had just received a much better present from my minister brother and his wife who had presented them with their first grandson.

A future rugby player? Moderator of the Church of Scotland? Prime Minister? He could be *anything*, a wonderful child like that, with five fingers on each hand and the same number of tootsies! And he would carry on the family name.

So, naturally, that pushed me and the Pyramids into the background. I went and examined the five fingers and toes myself, and made gooey noises at the infant who gave me an old-fashioned look as if to say, 'Talk sense, wumman!'

Then I kept my promise and went to visit Jessie.

I expected that she, too, would cut me down to size, but surprisingly she said, 'Weel done, lassie!' I felt a flush coming to my cheeks as she pointed to the local paper, the *Jedburgh Gazette* which we always called the Jethart Squeaker, where there was an item headed 'Local Lass Makes Good'. There was a fuzzy picture which might have been anybody and a write-up saying I had been chosen specially by a well-known publishing firm to represent them in Egypt. Fancy that!

I think the last time I appeared in The Squeaker was when I won second prize in the egg-and-spoon race at the School Sports. On that occasion all Jessie said was 'Huh!' Now she seemed genuinely pleased and it was *her* praise that mattered, not The Squeaker's.

I tried to tell her a little about my adventures, but she soon lost interest and asked about Phemie instead, wanting to know what was going on in the farmhouse kitchen now that it was no longer under *her* control.

'Oh Jessie! It's not the same without you,' I told her. True enough! I missed Jessie, of course, but the kitchen was now a more peaceful place, with Phemie getting through the work at her own pace and not being constantly harassed. I changed the subject and asked, 'How are you, Jessie?'

'Och! I'm fine,' she said sturdily.

'F-f-fine!' stuttered her sister, Joo-anne. Jock-the-herd, their brother, was sitting by the fire in his stocking-soles, painstakingly polishing the handle of a shepherd's crook. I admired his work and said, 'There was nothing like *that* in the shops in Cairo. You could make your fortune there, Jock.'

'Man-lassie!' grunted Jock. 'What wad *I* do wi' a fortune?'

True! The only reward Jock wanted was the satisfaction of knowing he had produced a fine crook, and that the long hours he had spent carving, whittling, honing and sandpapering had not been in vain.

Hold on! That's just what *I* want, I told

myself. If I could follow Jock's example and try to hone, carve, whittle and polish my stories I might learn, as he had done, to perfect my craft.

But first I must return to Glasgow and complete the tasks for the people who were employing me. The Egyptian episode vanished like snow off a dyke when I was summoned once more to partake of Mrs Marzipan's puddings in the boardroom.

'What now?' I thought warily, wondering if I was to be banished to the North or South Pole.

It was neither. The Directors came straight out with it even before the soup was served. This time it was a Rush Job (oh! those rush jobs!) of great importance which no one in the firm – or in the world – could do better or quicker than myself. I would be given every facility while doing the work. Anything I needed, I had only to ask and I would get it. And if I completed the job in time I would have a special trip to Holland where the book was to be printed. And could I start at once? Even before I had finished my soup?

'But what is it?' I asked fearfully.

It was a children's picture dictionary from *A* to *Z*.

I had imagined there were only twenty-six letters in the alphabet, but by the time I completed the dictionary (yes! on time, though the trip to Holland was forgotten by then) I was convinced there were hundreds if not thousands. *S* was the worst. I thought I would have to live with *it* for ever; and felt a great deal of sympathy for Dr Johnson as I ploughed wearily on, day after day after day.

Now that they had secured their victim the Directors, of course, forgot all about their fine promises till on the coldest day in February – which happened also to be my birthday – I was sitting shivering in the empty room allocated to me, puzzling my brains over a particularly tricky item when the door burst open and Good old Billy breezed in.

'Good Lord!' he cried, appalled at the sight of me wrapped up in a rug and with woollen gloves on my frozen fingers. 'Is there no heating in this room?'

I shook my head and stifled a sneeze, whereupon he said, 'Hold on! I'll see to it,' and dived out of the room. In less than five minutes, I had *two* electric fires going full blast and before long was dripping with perspiration.

The Collins family never did things by halves! They could be penny-pinching one moment and over-generous the next. Saving pencils, they seemed to think, would solve every economic problem. They themselves would scribble with blunt stubs; and their writing, indecipherable at the best of times, was as difficult to understand as the hieroglyphics on the Rosetta stone. But *they* knew, and were incensed when the rest of us were too stupid to guess their meaning.

But times were changing. The war had been a great leveller and the old autocratic method of ruling the roost was not so meekly accepted by the returning warriors who demanded their say as well as a bigger share of the cake.

The unions became more powerful and there was even the hint of a strike on one occasion. More up-to-date machinery was installed, and a fearsome monster called Hollerith (which, of course, was nicknamed *Hell*erith) became the firm's first computer system. Now it took twice as long to do half the work, with many mistakes snarling up the works. It was all in the name of progress.

'Progress!' scoffed a disillusioned worker. 'That brute's had mair teething troubles than ma weans.'

Some things remained the same. Clever though the computer was, its skills did not extend to automatic story writing. So I still had to conjure up my tales from the dusty recesses of my mind and write them down in the old-fashioned way. Instead of collecting rejections I was now being *asked* for contributions, so my pen was busy both at home and at the office. And from not knowing a single soul when I first came to my adopted city, I now seemed to know the entire population of Glasgow, all of them wanting me to *do* something.

Could you give a talk to the Old People's Club? Reply to the toast to the Lasses at a Burns Supper? Present the prizes at the Junior School? Join this or that Club? Tell us how to get a book published? How can we learn to make a speech?

The answer to *that* (get up, speak up, and shut up) came after much blood, sweat, and tears. First I had to learn to do it myself after painfully overcoming the terrors of standing up in public and facing an audience. I had already gone through my baptism of fire as a Lady of the Manse and come to the conclusion that it was not modesty but *im*modesty that caused reluctant speakers to shrink from facing an audience: Who do you think you are? Nobody's going to take any notice of you! You're not *that* important!

But, 'Oh no!' they protest. 'Me make a speech! No, no, I couldn't! I'm far too shy. It's nothing to you. You can do it standing on your head.'

So they never took the pains to get over that first hurdle. 'Oh no, I couldn't! But I'll sit back and listen to you if you come to our annual dinner and reply to the toast of the Guests. I wouldn't enjoy a bite of the dinner if *I* had to speak afterwards. You go ahead . . .' In other words, I'll sit back and watch *you* going through purgatory.

And it *was* purgatory to begin with; but I did my best to overcome my nerves and accepted a few invitations to 'oblige' people who were desperate for speakers. In some cases I received very off-hand treatment. 'You won't mind waiting in the corridor till we finish our committee meeting? We'll call you in when we're ready.' Was this worse, I wondered, than to sit listening to their long deliberations and then to be told by the Chairman: 'I'm afraid we've over-run a bit. Could you cut your talk to ten minutes? What did you say the subject was?'

Others flattered me by saying they 'could have listened all night', and my head might have been turned had I not guessed they were only filling in gaps in their calendar. 'She'll do! We must tell

Rotary about her. They could fit her in. Good! That's another date settled!'

I rationed my appearances though I found it difficult not to be persuaded by subtle flattery. 'I know I can depend on you. You'll do it for *my* sake, won't you? You'll be a great draw. Last month we had Mr X and he emptied the hall, but someone said you could fill it. I'm afraid there's no fee, but it's in a good cause . . .'

Now that I was comfortably settled in that small flat near the Botanic Gardens and 'doing for myself' I could invite friends for a Glasgow high tea or for supper. I used to race home from the office, light the fire (which I had laid in the morning before leaving), set the table, whip up a concoction of some kind in the kitchen, bake a scone if I had time, and have everything ready just in advance of my guests' arrival. I was accustomed to hurry-skurrying, but I sometimes wished I had more time for my real work – writing.

So that was why I became an employer myself in a small way and acquired a once-a-week cleaning-woman.

Mrs McThingummy.

She was far too good for me. She told me so herself, and I wondered if I could ever live up to her. Certainly my tatty scrubbing-brush couldn't. I hastened to buy a new one and the special brand of floor polish she fancied. 'And I hope you've got a cushion for my knees if I have to go down on them,' she said in her genteel voice.

But I never felt I could ask her to do anything

as menial, and found myself working twice as hard to save her doing the dirty jobs. As it happened, we did not meet very often but communicated by means of scribbled 'messages' left on the kitchen table. I was careful to make mine extra polite. 'Would you kindly wash out the bath, please? And I'd be very grateful if you could clean the oven. Thank you very much.'

She replied with a scrawl on a grocer's paperbag. 'I've did my best. The bowel broke.' (Referring to a baking bowl left in pieces on the kitchen table.) 'It just fell oot ma hand. You need more Vim.' (How true!)

Her real name was Mrs McTurk but it was ages before I caught on to it, so I just called her Mrs McThingummy to myself. In time I became quite fond of her. She was better than nobody, and when she saw I treated *her* like a lady, she treated me more or less like a human being. Whenever we met, I let her babble on like the brook. She had no one to talk to at home, she told me, except Bobby the budgie, and the pair of them seemed to chatter to each other from morning till night.

The first I knew about *him* was on the day she startled me by asking, 'D'you mind if I bring Bobby with me? He's great company and it's awful lonely here all by myself.'

'But will he not be in the way?' I said, thinking she must be referring to her husband, though I was not sure of the existence of a Mr McThingummy.

'Och no!' she scoffed. 'I'll keep him in his cage and he'll not be in nobody's way.'

For one awful moment I had visions of a henpecked Mr McTurk being shut up in a cage all day (and I wouldn't have put it past her) but when the light dawned on me, I had to say, 'Oh well!' – and that was it.

I made a point of being at home on her next visit, so that I could meet the talkative budgie, but to my disappointment he looked just like an ordinary wee bird and seldom got a word in edgeways, for it was Mrs McThingummy who did all the talking. But there were times when she put words into his beak. 'Bobby was saying,' she would begin, and I knew the budgie thought it was time we had some more washing-up liquid or a new carpet-sweeper.

But in spite of her peculiarities, she was loyal and trustworthy; and I was lucky to have her, she told me, adding darkly, 'You should see some!'

# 16. The World My Oyster

Now that I had conquered Abroad, I felt I could
fly to the Moon if the firm suggested another
free trip; but as none was forthcoming I had to
go off on my own steam to explore another
corner of the globe.

My first adventure started on the river Clyde
in a ship called the *Esja*. It was bound for a
mysterious place called Iceland and the passengers were to live on board when the ship anch-
ored in Reykjavik. If it ever reached that length.

I had never heard of stabilizers; neither had the
good ship *Esja*. And she must have been a *good*
ship, else she would never have withstood the
buffeting we got when we reached the open sea
and the storm struck. I have to report with some
complacency that I enjoyed every moment of it.

For the first time in my life I discovered I was

a good sailor. This was no credit to me but to *my* in-built stabilizers; so while others took to their bunks and longed for death, I stayed on board pitching and tossing with the ship and hanging on to the rails as the spray swept over me.

A gruff sailor pulled me away and ordered me down to the cabin I shared with an English lady called Vera Somebody. She wore her hair in earphones and had been very prim when I met her first. Now she had lost all dignity. Her earphones were tousled out of shape and she could only moan: 'Stop the ship! Go away! Stop the ship! Go away . . .'

I went away but I couldn't stop the ship. By chance I stumbled into the dining-room and felt ashamed to be the only female sitting at a table trying to eat a ham roll. There were only two other diners in the room, stalwart men who were having difficulty catching their cutlery as it sprang up and danced in midair. The fiddles were up, but yet the plates trundled over the side. Through it all I steadily consumed my ham roll, even when I landed on the floor and ate it more or less upside down.

Indeed, for a day and a night the whole ship seemed to be upside down, and some of the crew – Icelanders and Glaswegians alike – were as sick as the passengers. I achieved some sort of Florence Nightingale reputation by answering distress calls from various cabins. 'He-e-lp! I'm dying!' I held sundry hands and brows, later brought tea and toast to the stricken, and even helped Vera Somebody do up her earphones when she began to recover.

Suddenly the sea was as calm as a millpond. The *Esja* glided along like a swan, and the passengers, their ordeal forgotten, emerged from their cabins wearing shorts and sunhats.

Two young men from Switzerland, Fritz and Jakob, to whom I had ministered, were so grateful they adopted me and presented me with bars of Swiss chocolate from a hoard they had brought from Berne. It was so delicious and I ate it so rapidly I was in danger of being choc-sick though I had avoided being sea-sick.

The entire population of Reykjavik came out to the harbour to welcome us. Flags were flying and all the ships bedecked; but it was not a special occasion. It was just that the harbour was a focal point, a meeting-place for the islanders who strolled about in little groups watching the comings and goings.

It was difficult to tell whether it was midday or midnight for the light seemed equally bright at any time of day and no one ever appeared to get tired. Even I, who had scarcely closed an eye since I left the Clyde, felt buoyed up and ready to stay awake for ever – till I went on shore with the Swiss lads who set up their tent on a grassy knoll near the harbour. I christened it Swiss Cottage, and when I went inside to examine it, sat down on one of their sleeping-bags – and suddenly I was not there . . .

Fritz and Jakob did not waken me till they had brewed a pot of tea and revived me with a plastic mug full of the strong sweet drink. Even so, it took me a long time to get out of my daze and adjust to life in a topsy-turvy land where the natives never went to bed.

They seemed amiable enough – the natives – though on the whole not communicative, not surprising since we had no common tongue. Not even *loud* French brought any reply. The Swiss Cottagers tried them with German which some-times brought a flicker of reply, but mostly we gesticulated as if semaphoring our conversation.

The Swiss were good companions and though I did not always understand them, or they me, we laughed a lot which one can do in any language. And somehow or other, I managed to discover a few facts about Iceland; that it was not such an icy land when roses could bloom in December, thanks to its hot springs, and that luscious fruits could be produced all the year round in the hothouses. I watched the springs bubbling up from the bare ground, saw a whale being flensed (and the water turning into a Red Sea of blood), explored the interior of the country, travelling on bumpy un-tarmacadamed roads; and even climbed a volcanic mountain.

This was a foolhardy expedition urged on me by the persuasive Swiss chaps who were accus-tomed to running up and down an Alp without turning a hair. *They* were real climbers and had all the right gear, but *I* set out in my sandshoes wearing a summery frock.

The mountain was 'Esja', the same name as our ship. It was a mere nothing to my companions, though in reality a tricky enough climb for it had a habit of erupting when least expected. I don't know if I was hot or cold when I started the ascent, but I boiled and froze at the same time when I felt the shifting lava under my feet beginning to smoke.

It was only cooling down from a previous eruption, the Swiss told me, and urged me to hurry up. I had no breath left to speak back, so I had to plod onwards and upwards. Upwards was a painful process.

All I could see were Fritz's boots several steps ahead of me. Occasionally he and Jakob set off a shoal of crumbling stones which trundled down on top of me, almost sweeping me off my feet. It was difficult to find a foothold on such treacherous terrain, and suddenly I became catatonic and knew I could not go one step further. So I stuck there like a stookie; all I longed for was another eruption to put me out of my misery.

Fritz and Jakob slid down to my side and spoke sternly to me. I got the gist of their message! What they did with folk like me (not that they had met any as bad) was to slap them hard on the face. Like this! They showed me how they would do it. *Slap! Slap! SLAP!* And they looked so fierce I thought they meant to carry out their threat there and then.

The ruse worked! *Force* your feet to move, I told myself. Anything would be better than the indignity of being slapped in the face. The Swiss Cottagers held out helping hands and inch by inch hauled me to the top. I sank down on the warm lava feeling neither pain nor pleasure. Eventually I looked around me and beheld a wonderful sight: the whole world stretched out before my eyes. There was no end to it. On all sides it went on for ever and ever, and the air was so pure I felt I would go off pop like a cork out of a bottle.

It was easier going down. I just slipped and slithered, sometimes on my sandshoes, sometimes on my bottom, and landed in a crumpled heap at the foot *before* the real mountaineers had made a proper descent.

I am ashamed to confess that by the time I got back to Glasgow, though still bruised and battered, I had begun to brag about it.

'Oh yes! I climbed Esja. Uh-huh! Right to the top. No, no! It was no bother . . .'

Oh Jessie! What has happened to your truthful lassie?

I have remained on friendly terms with the Swiss Cottagers over the years, and have gone on several visits to see the bears of Berne and have a look at their snowcapped mountains. I have even gone up the Jungfrau (the easy way in a funicular). Fritz and Jakob twinkled their eyes at me and said: 'Better fun climbing Esja!'

Hm!

And now as a member of the PEN Club I was given the opportunity to attend gatherings of writers at conferences in different parts of the globe: real writers of international fame. I felt both proud and humble when I was first chosen to be a delegate of Scottish PEN to attend a Congress in Dublin, along with Nigel Tranter. Nigel was already an established author with some fifty books to his credit, and showed no awe of Peter Ustinov or Rose Macaulay, or even of de Valera when he welcomed us to a grand gathering in Phoenix Park.

De Valera's eyesight was so poor that when he peered at my delegate's badge he could not make out which country I came from, so I helped him by saying in my broad tongue: 'I'm from Scotland.'

'Ah!' said he, pumping my hand up and down. 'So you come from the land of the kilt. Weel done, lassie!'

Apart from the interest of meeting eminent writers and dignitaries, I was fascinated with Dublin itself, which was chockful of stage characters. I could have stood on one of the Liffey bridges and watched them for ages, or listened to the cadences of their voices as I browsed amongst the bookstalls on the quayside. ('Goodness! There's a Collins book I helped to edit.') They were not merely passing the time of day. They were talking to each other about matters of the mind. Though some of them were in rags their heads seemed to be full of poetry, and I felt *they* could have taken honourable places at any of the literary sessions I was attending.

Years later when I met the Quare Fella – Brendan Behan – I found he had the same appreciation of words and how to put them together, in between all his rampaging and blaspheming. The trouble was to get him to sit still long enough to think. 'Ach! Come on to the boozer,' he would say restlessly.

In a pub the Fella became too much of a handful for me so I had a habit of disappearing into thin air while he was having a heated discussion with one of his cronies. But I attended a gathering held in his favourite 'howf' after his funeral, in company with his wife Beatrice, his gallant old mother, and many of his faithful friends, one of whom was a larger than life character called Petronella O'Flannigan.

Petra worked in Radio Eireann and thought my funny tongue would fascinate her listeners – I thought *her* tongue was funny, too – and for many years I broadcast regularly from RE in a hit-or-miss fashion. What would Auntie Kathleen at the BBC have thought of it! There was always a supply of what the director called 'holy water' on hand with which he tried to regale me before I faced the microphone; but 'Oh, no, no!' I said pushing it aside. 'I'll manage without!'

On that first visit I discovered the delights of a succulent sweetmeat called 'Peggy's Leg' and sampled some of the chocolate biscuits that were unrationed. The sight of shops full of goodies unobtainable back home went to my head, as did the availability of twin-sets which could be purchased without relinquishing a single coupon. I went through purgatory trying to smuggle two woollen jerseys through the customs on the way home. How I escaped detection I'll never know, with my guilty countenance and the sweat pouring off my brow. I was wearing both garments under my regular garb, and suffered so much mentally and physically that I concluded I was not cut out for a life of crime.

It was interesting to discover that even the great authors present were human enough to be peevish about their publishers or to have writers' blocks; but mostly they talked about writing in a general way, not, thank goodness, hogging every conversation with long gabbles about 'my' latest book: 'My agent tells me it's going to be a best seller. I have a feeling he's right!'

Never, never, NEVER be tempted, I warned myself. Just shut up and listen.

Oh! What a pleasure it was to listen to Patricia Lynch who was present at the Congress with her husband, R. M. Fox. I had read and revelled in *A Turf-Cutter's Donkey*. And *there* was the author herself looking as if she never strayed from a gypsy encampment or used any other transport than a donkey. When she invited me to tea in a house on the outskirts of Dublin (and what a job I had to find it) I discovered a real turf fire and Patricia sitting by it looking more at home than she did at the Congress.

Jessie would have been appalled at the clutter in the crowded kitchen, the unswept hearth, the year-old dust on the mantel-shelf and the kettle spitting over on to the rug. Patricia and R. M. produced some sandwiches for tea. Luckily I was not much of an eater, for had I been starving I could not have consumed the mouldy offerings which must have been made days if not weeks before.

It did not matter. I drank the tea and Patricia fed me with much better fare when she began to talk in her lilting voice about leprechauns and little people. I felt I was back in the byre listening to Jessie spinning her tales as she milked the cows. In the heat of the turf fire I began to nod off, and had to pull myself together to get back to town in time to dress myself in a long gown to wear at a reception in Dublin Castle.

It was a white gown, which my fellow delegates deemed 'Not bad': and as we assembled in the courtyard one of a group of urchins, gazing at us, said in an awe-struck voice: 'Aw! See the quality!'

So that was what we were. Quality! All evening in my white gown I could not take my mind off that ragged little group, and longed to run out to them with handfuls of the goodies that were being lavished on us inside the Castle. Though I was assured the urchins were not envious, only excited at seeing such strange apparitions, the smoked salmon left a bad taste in my mouth, and I wished I was back at Patricia Lynch's fireside.

I sent a picture postcard of the Castle to Mrs McTurk who 'obliged' me, feeling such grandeur might impress her; but to Jessie I sent one of a jaunting-car and wrote in big letters: 'This reminds me of the gig we had at home. Remember how often I fell out!' I could almost hear her reply: 'Ay, lassie! I dinna ken how ye ever grew up!'

I found castles in Scotland, too, and when I got home I was invited to stay in one by a new acquaintance who was to become a staunch friend. Naomi Mitchison was not everyone's cup of tea. She called a spade a spade, had no time for poseurs, but possessed more brains in her wee pinky than most of her detractors had in their entire bodies.

The castle was a rambling edifice in Kintyre, Argyllshire, which Naomi – or Nou, as her friends called her – shared with her husband, the politician Dick Mitchison (later to become Lord Mitchison) and a squad of children and friends as a holiday home. It was always bursting at the seams, and introductions were not *de rigeur* so who was who had to be found out furtively. It was like feeling one's way in the dark, or like finding out the location of the few bathrooms in the castle!

We came down to breakfast at any hour and helped ourselves from the sideboard or wandered through to the kitchen to prepare our own dishes. So there were great comings and goings between those about to fry a kipper and others fetching a second helping of porridge. I found myself assisting a black gentleman from Botswana to make toast (Nou collected guests from all over the world) while George – *he* turned out to be Lord Somebody – wanted to know how to scramble a duck's egg.

Somehow we all got fed satisfactorily and went about our own business. Nobody asked anybody what they wanted to do. It was left to ourselves to get on with it. But as the day progressed life became more formal, culminating in a great dressing-up at night when we all assembled for dinner.

In time I became Dick's right-hand man, always sitting beside him at table, helping him to open his mail when the Postie came in to deliver it in the morning, and accompanying him to the cellar at night to choose (not that I knew much about it) the right vintage to drink with venison, salmon or any other of the food on the night's menu.

Both he and Nou had large desks in the spacious sitting-room, and when we all assembled to enjoy the comfort of a roaring log fire, they sat working – Nou writing her current book, Dick perhaps preparing a parliamentary speech or doing his income tax – still keeping a listening ear on the company so that they could contribute their quota to the conversation.

When Naomi became Lady Mitchison she paid little attention to the honour, but my Mrs McTurk thought the better of me for having such a highly bred friend, and when Nou came to stay bobbed her a curtsey before asking, 'Would you prefair tea or coffee, your ladyship? It's all the one!'

It was great to feel that *I* had gone up in the world.

But my heart was still in the Borders where *real* people lived. The rest were only mirages.

Sometimes I wondered if *I* was real myself or only a figment of my own imagination. As time went by I saw someone on the television screen wearing a frock similar to one I had in my wardrobe. The brooch at the neck was surely one Santa had brought *me* at Christmas. And what was that faintly familiar figure talking about?

Jessie!

Yes! she was telling of the time she sat on a stool in the byre listening to Jessie spinning her stories. It was all so familiar and yet all so unreal . . .

Could that be *me* on the screen?

# *Envoi*

In the distance I could hear the strains of a familiar tune: the *Blue Danube*.

Ta-tum! Ta-tum! TA!

Soon it would reach the crack on the record and I would have to lift the arm to prevent the music from sticking. Maybe if I hunted high and low I could find a better needle to improve the sound.

Ta-tum! Ta-tum! TA!

To my surprise the music played on without stopping; and even without a new needle the *Blue Danube* was becoming louder and more melodious. It made me want to whirl away in a roundabout waltz with Jock-the-herd as a partner. Man-lassie! Steady on!

Ta-tum! Ta-tum!

Suddenly I realized I was not in the farmhouse

kitchen at home, with the old gramophone creaking its way through its repertoire of damaged records. I was in much grander surroundings.

*Buckingham Palace.*

It was the band of the Irish Guards that was changing its tune to *We'll Gather Lilacs* as I neared the open door of the ballroom. I glimpsed a glittering chandelier, and a posse of people on a dais with the Yeomen of the Guard protecting a small dignified figure.

*Her Majesty the Queen!*

When my name was called out I would have to march forward, turn and face the monarch, then curtsey. It was too late now. There was no going back . . .

When I first received the official letter inviting me to become an MBE (Member of the British Empire) I was so stunned I did not tell anyone, not even my china dogs. For days I fluctuated between Yes and No; then when time was running out sent a hasty acceptance. Forget about it, I told myself. The day might never come – so I pushed it into the background of unthinkable thoughts.

Indeed, I thought so little about it *I* was amongst those who were surprised when the official announcement was made. Help! It had really happened! But once again I shoved the whole matter into that limbo of never-never-ness. Until I received a summons to present myself at Buckingham Palace.

This was it!

I must put my best foot forward and buy some

suitable garments for the occasion. A well-meaning friend advised me not to be drab, so I chose a rose-pink outfit, not knowing that Her Majesty would be similarly attired on the great day. (Though hers, of course, was of superior quality!) Black hat, black shoes, black gloves and accessories and I was all set, except for a rose-pink ribbon to cheer up my plain hat.

I bought it in London just as the shops were closing on the night before the ceremony. I had come to London in advance and was having a session with my literary agent.

He was vastly amused when I rushed off saying, 'Must catch the shops! I have to go to the Palace tomorrow.'

He was astounded at my nonchalance, but it did not last. Suddenly, as I was dressing in my hotel bedroom next morning, I was poleaxed with terror. I was fully clothed, with my dressing-gown on top of my finery, and my hat with the pink ribbon perched on my head. All ready to set off to Buckingham Palace.

Me!

My knees suddenly turned to jelly. What had I let myself in for? I was not prepared to meet Her Majesty. I had not even practised my curtsey. So, with my carpet-slippers still on my feet, I advanced and retired, curtseying to my own reflection in the dressing-table mirror.

I was becoming quite good at it – backwards and forwards – when suddenly I heard a burst of applause, and whipping round caught sight of two window-cleaners grinning at me from outside. Scarlet-faced, I rushed and hid in the bathroom till they had gone – and that was the end of my rehearsal.

Now here I was, booted and spurred, progressing sedately in line towards my monarch. I had got over my fear and lost all feeling by now. I was merely a mechanical robot. Eyes front! Left foot forward; right foot forward! Don't stumble! You're getting nearer! The music is louder . . . *We'll Gather Lilacs* . . . Your name is being called . . .

Was that Jessie's voice speaking to me from the past? 'Heid up, lassie! Shoulders back! Best foot forward!'

Turn and face her Majesty. Mercy! She's wearing *my* frock! Curtsey– Oh, not bad! She's speaking to you! Answer her! 'Yes, ma'am!' Walk away. Backwards! Don't fall down, and don't rush now that it's all over.

You've done it and you're still alive.

'Isn't it terrible?' A distinguished-looking lady in uniform was bemoaning the fact that, in her confusion, she had turned her back on the Queen. 'I was so flustered. Oh dear! What will she think of me?'

'Och! She'd never notice,' I said airily, feeling perky because *I* had not disgraced myself. I took the medal off my chest and tucked it away in its wee box. I could get a little replica to wear on special occasions.

But what would I do with the original?

I was already mentally packing up the trophy and composing a note to go with it.

'It's yours, Jessie! I could never have earned it if you hadn't taught me rummlegumption. Thanks!'

bathroom till they had gone – and that was the end of my rehearsal.

Now here I was, booted and spurred, progressing sedately in line towards my monarch. I had got over my fear and lost all feeling by now. I was merely a mechanical robot. Eyes front! Left foot forward; right foot forward! Don't stumble! You're getting nearer! The music is louder . . . *We'll Gather Lilacs* . . . Your name is being called . . .

Was that Jessie's voice speaking to me from the past? 'Heid up, lassie! Shoulders back! Best foot forward!'

Turn and face her Majesty. Mercy! She's wearing *my* frock! Curtsey– Oh, not bad! She's speaking to you! Answer her! 'Yes, ma'am!' Walk away. Backwards! Don't fall down, and don't rush now that it's all over.

You've done it and you're still alive.

'Isn't it terrible?' A distinguished-looking lady in uniform was bemoaning the fact that, in her confusion, she had turned her back on the Queen. 'I was so flustered. Oh dear! What will she think of me?'

'Och! She'd never notice,' I said airily, feeling perky because *I* had not disgraced myself. I took the medal off my chest and tucked it away in its wee box. I could get a little replica to wear on special occasions.

But what would I do with the original?

I was already mentally packing up the trophy and composing a note to go with it.

'It's yours, Jessie! I could never have earned
it if you hadn't taught me rummlegumption.
Thanks!'